AI-Driven

Transformation

of the SOC and SecOps

2nd edition

by

Adeel Shaikh Muhammad

Contents

Acknowledgments

All praise and thanks are due to Allah, who has blessed me with the strength, curiosity, and resilience to complete this book. Writing this has been nothing short of a journey — one filled with late nights, countless cups of coffee, and moments of both frustration and revelation. None of it would have been possible without the grace of Allah, and for that, my gratitude knows no limits.

To my beloved parents, your unwavering love, prayers, and support have been my greatest blessings. You have instilled in me the values of faith, dedication, and hard work, and for that, I am eternally grateful. May Allah reward you for all that you have done for me.

To my dear wife, your patience deserves an award. Thank you for believing in me and for not changing the locks when I was buried in work. May Allah bless you for your sacrifices and the countless cups of coffees you brought me.

To my little champ, thank you for being so patient while Dad was busy writing this book instead of playing with you. I know it wasn't easy to understand why I was always glued to the computer, but your bright smile and playful energy kept me going. I promise we'll have plenty of playtime to make up for it – maybe even an extra scoop of ice cream or two. May Allah reward you with endless blessings and fun.

To my family, friends, and teachers who have been a source of encouragement and wisdom, I offer my heartfelt thanks. Your advice, prayers, and support have been instrumental in the completion of this work.

And to you, the reader—whether you're a seasoned SOC leader or a curious analyst trying to make sense of the chaos – thank you for trusting me with your time. I hope this book becomes a companion, a guide, and maybe even a mirror reflecting the challenges you face daily. May it serve as a small step toward smarter, calmer, and more human-centered cybersecurity.

Foreword (Author's Note)

I've always wondered — why is cybersecurity so complicated? Why are there countless vendors, each offering a slice of the puzzle, yet no single, unified approach that truly simplifies security? In an ideal world, there would be something like Cybersecurity-as-a-Service, an all-encompassing solution that eliminates complexity and streamlines protection. But reality is far messier.

When I set out to explore this challenge, I quickly realized the sheer magnitude of the problem. The cybersecurity landscape is vast, evolving at breakneck speed, and tackling it would have meant writing a 600+ page book — one that even the most dedicated security professionals might struggle to finish. Instead, I decided to focus on the Security Operations Center (SOC) — the backbone of modern cybersecurity. If we can simplify and optimize the SOC, we can redefine how security teams operate, bringing us one step closer to a future where security is more effective, less complex, and truly AI-driven.

This book is deeply tied to my own doctoral research, where I explored the impact of AI on SOC mechanisms, looking for ways to enhance and simplify security operations. Since publishing the first version, I have continued to refine my understanding and, more importantly, found real-world solutions that bring AI-driven security closer to reality. With this second edition, I am working together with Kindo, the AI-Native Security and Autonomous Infrastructure platform, to expand on these ideas and showcase how AI is transforming SOCs today. The emergence of platforms like Kindo (www.kindo.ai) and WhiteRabbitNeo has shown that automation, AI, and autonomous agents are not just buzzwords — they are the future of SOCs.

With this Version 2, I've refined my insights, incorporated the latest technological advancements, and made the book more practical, actionable, and forward-thinking. My goal remains the same:

To simplify cybersecurity, to break down the barriers that make SOC operations complex, and to inspire a shift towards AI-driven security that actually works.

I hope this book helps you navigate the evolving landscape of SOCs, embrace AI-powered security, and take steps toward a more efficient and resilient cybersecurity future.

Let's build a smarter, faster, and more autonomous SOC — together.

Adeel Shaikh Muhammad

Unlocking the AI-Powered SOC: A Sneak Peek into the Chapters

Before diving into the depths of AI-driven Security Operations Centers (SOCs), let's take a moment to explore what's ahead.

This section offers a high-level glimpse into each chapter, setting the stage for an exciting journey into how AI is reshaping cybersecurity.

Whether you're here to understand the flaws of traditional SOCs, explore AI's defensive and offensive capabilities, or uncover the ethical implications of automation, this book has something for you.

Buckle up—this is the future of security, and you're about to get a front-row seat.

Chapter One: Laying the Groundwork for AI-driven SOC

SOCs are at a turning point. AI isn't just a nice-to-have anymore: it's a game-changer. Before diving into the deep end, it's essential to understand how SOCs operate today, where they fall short, and why AI-driven solutions are becoming the backbone of modern security. This section sets the foundation, ensuring a smooth transition into the AI-powered future of cybersecurity.

Chapter Two: Why AI is a Thing in Cybersecurity

AI has officially entered the battlefield, and it's not going anywhere. From automating tedious security tasks to spotting threats in real-time, AI is revolutionizing cybersecurity at an unprecedented pace. But why is it such a big deal? This section unpacks how AI has evolved, why it's so effective in detecting threats, and how organizations are leveraging its capabilities to stay ahead of attackers.

Chapter Three: Why Traditional SOCs Are Losing Their Steeze

The old way of running a SOC is crumbling. Security teams are overwhelmed by alert fatigue, slow response times, and an ever-growing list of cyber threats. Meanwhile, attackers are moving faster than ever. The cracks in traditional SOC models are widening, and sticking to outdated methods is no longer an option. Here's a look at why the old ways don't cut it anymore and what's needed to fix them.

Chapter Four: The Rise of AI-Enhanced Threats

AI isn't just empowering defenders: it's also arming cybercriminals. Sophisticated phishing, deepfake-powered scams, and AI-driven malware are making cyberattacks harder to detect and even harder to stop. Attackers are using AI to move faster, remain undetected, and scale their operations like never before. Understanding how these AI-driven threats work the first step is toward defending against them.

Chapter Five: How AI Enhances Threat Detection

Imagine a security analyst that never gets tired, processes information at lightning speed, and instantly identifies real threats amid the noise. AI is that analyst. By using machine learning and behavioral analytics, AI enhances threat detection by eliminating false positives, recognizing anomalies, and responding to threats before they escalate. The days of drowning in alerts are over, AI is changing the game.

Chapter Six: How to Thrive with AI and Autonomous Agents

AI isn't just a tool; it's a teammate. SOCs that integrate AI with human expertise are seeing incredible gains in efficiency and effectiveness. Autonomous agents can take over repetitive tasks, freeing up analysts to focus on high-priority threats. But the key is knowing how to work alongside AI, leveraging its strengths without losing sight of human intuition.

Chapter Seven: Future Trends: AI-Enabled Security is an Ever-Evolving Landscape

Cybersecurity doesn't stand still, and neither does AI. The next wave of advancements will bring predictive defense models, fully autonomous SOCs, and even AI-powered cyber deception strategies. As technology continues to evolve, so do the threats. Staying ahead means keeping an eye on what's coming next and preparing for a future where AI isn't just part of security, it is security.

Chapter Eight: Predictive Analytics for Proactive Cyber Defense

Why wait for an attack when you can see it coming? Predictive analytics leverages AI to detect attack patterns before they manifest into full-blown breaches. By analyzing historical data and real-time behaviors, AI can forecast potential threats, allowing security teams to take a proactive stance rather than constantly playing defense.

Chapter Nine: Operational Efficiencies Through AI

Security operations have long been plagued by inefficiencies, too many alerts, too much manual work, and not enough automation. AI streamlines workflows, prioritizes incidents intelligently, and automates responses, making SOCs more efficient and effective. Analysts spend less time on false positives and more time on real threats, resulting in faster resolutions and a stronger security posture.

Chapter Ten: Ethical and Legal Implications of AI in SOCs

With great power comes great responsibility. AI's role in cybersecurity raises critical questions about privacy, accountability, and bias. How much control should AI have over security decisions? What happens when AI makes a mistake? Navigating the legal and ethical landscape of AI in cybersecurity is just as important as leveraging its technical capabilities.

Chapter Eleven: Human-Machine Collaboration in SOCs

It's not a competition between humans and AI: it's a partnership. The best security teams know how to integrate AI into their workflows while maintaining human oversight. By combining AI's analytical power with human intuition, SOCs can strike the perfect balance between automation and expert judgment, ensuring no critical decision is left entirely to machines.

Chapter Twelve: Implementing AI in SOCs: Best Practices

Knowing AI's potential is one thing but implementing it effectively is another. Successful AI adoption in SOCs requires a structured approach, from selecting the right tools to training analysts on how to work with AI-driven systems. Avoiding pitfalls and leveraging best practices can make the difference between an AI-enhanced SOC and one that struggles with integration.

Chapter One

Laying the Groundwork for AI-driven SOC

If you've ever spent a shift inside a Security Operations Center, you already know the unique mix of urgency, pressure, and information overload that defines life in those rooms. Screens blink constantly, alerts pile up faster than anyone can process, and somewhere in that sea of data, a real threat might be hiding.

The role of SOCs has evolved rapidly. Just a few years ago, traditional tools and methodologies were sufficient to manage threats. But today, the speed, complexity, and automation of cyberattacks have changed the game entirely. AI-driven threats now exploit vulnerabilities at machine speed, outpacing manual defenses and overwhelming analysts with more noise than clarity.

This realization is what led me to rewrite this book. I came up with the answer to all these problems—Kindo with WhiteRabbitNeo. The industry is in the midst of an AI explosion—every vendor is branding their tools as 'AI-driven,' yet SOCs are becoming more chaotic instead of more efficient. AI, when implemented improperly, increases alert fatigue, generates unnecessary noise, and places even greater strain on already overburdened teams. I have seen this firsthand, and I strongly believe that Kindo is not just another AI-labeled solution—it is redefining SOCs entirely. By eliminating outdated, ineffective legacy SOC models, Kindo is creating a new standard, one that is agile, intelligent, and capable of keeping pace with the evolving threat landscape. I strongly believe that Kindo is revolutionizing SOCs—eliminating ineffective legacy models and replacing them with a proactive, AI-driven approach that truly works. That's why I am reworking this second edition—to address these challenges head-on and demonstrate how AI, when applied correctly, can transform SOC operations rather than complicating them further.

The Rapid Evolution of Threats

Cyber threats have evolved dramatically over the past two decades. In the early 2000s, attacks were often the work of lone hackers defacing websites, spreading simple worms, or exploiting vulnerabilities for notoriety. By the 2010s, cybercrime became industrialized — organized groups deployed ransomware, banking trojans, and social engineering schemes for massive financial gain. State-sponsored actors entered the scene, targeting critical infrastructure and intellectual property. Then, in the 2020s, the game changed entirely.

Today, in 2025, AI-driven attacks have accelerated the threat landscape at an unprecedented pace. These aren't just automated exploits; they are adaptive, leveraging real-time data and advanced techniques to execute multi-layered, coordinated campaigns across diffuse attack surfaces. SOCs that were effective just three years ago are now struggling to keep up. AI has introduced a level of unpredictability that makes traditional SOC models feel obsolete almost overnight. If security teams don't evolve by integrating AI-driven automation and data-driven insights, they won't just fall behind: they will be left defenseless.

The Urgency of AI in SOCs

The past few years have shown that conventional SOCs, even with automation tools like SIEM and SOAR, are struggling to keep up. The sheer volume of alerts, false positives, and fragmented data streams creates an operational nightmare. The overall approach still relied heavily on human glue — analysts piecing things together by jumping between dashboards, correlating logs manually, and building playbooks reactively. Even well-resourced teams find themselves firefighting rather than proactively hunting threats.

What's needed is a fundamental shift — an AI-driven SOC that doesn't just generate more alerts but actively assists analysts in making faster, more accurate decisions. The goal isn't to replace analysts, but to augment their expertise, ensuring they can focus on investigation and strategy rather than drowning in repetitive tasks.

The Kindo and WhiteRabbitNeo Difference

This is where Kindo and WhiteRabbitNeo come in. Unlike traditional AI-labeled security solutions that add complexity without real efficiency gains, Kindo is built to truly transform

SOC operations. By leveraging Generative AI (GenAI) and deep contextual analysis, it filters out noise, prioritizes real threats, and enhances decision-making at every step. WhiteRabbitNeo, the first open-source, uncensored AI model built for DevSecOps teams, empowers security professionals with unprecedented insight and automation capabilities.

Together, these innovations redefine what an AI-driven SOC should look like—one that is proactive, adaptive, and efficient, ensuring analysts can operate at machine speed without losing control over security operations.

This book will explore that transformation—one step, one chapter at a time.

Traditional SOC Mechanisms and Their Limitations

Before we dissect traditional SOC mechanisms and their limitations, let's pause for a moment to reflect on what a SOC actually is—and why its role is so crucial in modern cybersecurity. By now, "SOC" is probably a term you've seen in countless conversations, presentations, and job descriptions. But what does it truly mean? And more importantly, why does its evolution matter now more than ever?

A Security Operations Center is essentially the nerve center of an organization's cybersecurity defenses. It is a centralized command hub that coordinates threat detection, response, and recovery — all under one roof, with analysts monitoring and defending the environment 24/7. Think of it as cybersecurity's version of air traffic control, where every log, alert, and anomaly pass through a vigilant team of analysts, working in shifts, to ensure threats are intercepted before they cause harm.

This concept of a centralized security team makes perfect sense, especially in today's complex and hyper-connected world. But here's the uncomfortable truth, the traditional mechanisms that SOCs rely on were built for a different era. They were designed for less data, simpler networks, and slower attacks. And that's exactly why, when faced with the speed and sophistication of today's threats, these approaches crumble under pressure.

The biggest flaw in traditional SOCs isn't that they lack smart people, it's that they rely too heavily on manual processes. In the past, analysts would manually monitor and review logs, combing through alerts one by one, hoping to spot the needle in the haystack before it turned into a breach. This may have worked a decade ago, when logs were counted in the thousands. But today? SOCs receive millions of logs and thousands of alerts every day, across cloud, on-prem, and hybrid environments, generated by dozens of overlapping tools.

As I observed this reality across multiple organizations, one pattern became clear, the sheer volume of data has outgrown human capacity to process it. Analysts aren't failing because they aren't skilled; they're failing because manual processes were never meant to handle this scale. Imagine asking air traffic controllers to manage every flight manually. That's exactly what many SOC analysts face today — and the results are predictable: missed alerts, delayed responses, and dangerous burnout.

But it's not just volume that's the problem. Traditional SOC tools often generate overwhelming numbers of false positives. Analysts are buried under a mountain of alerts, most of which are meaningless noise, leaving them with little time to focus on the actual threats that matter. This flood of irrelevant data isn't just frustrating — it's dangerous, because it desensitizes analysts. The more noise they sift through, the more likely they are to miss the subtle signs of a real attack.

To make matters worse, each security tool speaks its own language. The SIEM, the EDR, the NDR, the XDR, the SOAR, the deception solutions, the threat intelligence platforms, they all generate alerts in different formats, requiring analysts to translate, correlate, and cross-reference data manually - integrations are messy and not easy. This fragmented approach is slow, error-prone, and exhausting. And when fatigue sets in (as it inevitably does) mistakes become inevitable.

It's in this backdrop that I began exploring how modern SOCs could break free from the manual trap that has crippled their effectiveness for years. After evaluating several approaches and tools, I found that Kindo emerged as the clear answer to these challenges. What stood out about Kindo was its ability to directly address the root causes of SOC fatigue — not by adding yet another isolated tool, but by automating complex analysis, drastically reducing false positives through intelligent correlation, and seamlessly unifying data from multiple security layers into a single, clear narrative. In my professional view, Kindo doesn't just improve the SOC — it redefines how the SOC operates, enabling security teams to work smarter, respond faster, and see the full picture without drowning in noise.

This isn't about replacing the human analyst — it's about enabling the human analyst to thrive in a world where threats move faster than humans ever could. And that's the shift modern SOCs must embrace if they hope to keep up with attackers who already use automation and AI to their advantage.

Another serious limitation in traditional SOCs isn't necessarily a lack of threat intelligence — but how that intelligence is managed, processed, and applied. Threat intelligence, at its core, is one of the most valuable weapons a SOC can have. It's like early radar warning, collecting global signals about emerging attack patterns, new malware variants, vulnerable systems, and the shifting tactics of threat actors.

In theory, this should give analysts a powerful advantage — seeing threats before they hit. But in practice, most traditional SOCs drown in this flood of data. Security teams subscribe to multiple feeds, each delivering mountains of indicators, threat reports, and contextual alerts. Platforms like Anomali, ThreatQuotient, or Recorded Future can certainly enhance visibility, but they all add to the analyst's workload. Each new feed brings its own format, taxonomy, and prioritization rules—leaving analysts to manually correlate intelligence with real-time alerts and internal telemetry.

This manual stitching process is where traditional SOCs falter. Intelligence isn't lacking time and processing power are. By the time analysts connect the dots, the threat may already have breached the perimeter. This transforms threat intelligence from a proactive asset into a reactive scramble—used only after an incident to explain what went wrong, instead of preventing the incident in the first place.

This was one of the factors that led me to explore modern tools designed to automate the integration of threat intelligence into live workflows. One thing I appreciated about Kindo is how it doesn't treat threat intelligence as a standalone data point but integrates it seamlessly into the detection and response process, automatically correlating external intelligence with internal events giving analysts actionable context in real time, rather than another pile of disconnected reports. A tool like Kindo, that allows analysts to create agents to monitor logs from your entire security stack, is needed to cut through all of the noise and connect the various reports.

Furthermore, with Kindo and security-trained AI models, the days of hoping that your rigid deterministic pattern matching SIEM query is asking the right question to reveal a pattern you cannot see are over. Instead, analysts can now use natural language and AI's ability to semantically understand the endless variations of how meaning is conveyed via text to uncover emerging threats more intuitively. This is further enhanced by the recent AI advance of "reasoning" which empowers the latest open-source AI models to think through various possible causes and effects. A traditional query like "failed login attempts over the past 24 hours by source IP" often returns limited insights but remains necessary. However, with Kindo, analysts can instead ask, "Are there any unusual spikes in failed logins across multiple accounts that could indicate an attack?" This shift provides instant context and nuance, allowing analysts to make informed decisions as they monitor, prioritize, and mitigate threats in real time.

Another structural weakness of traditional SOCs is their limited scalability. As organizations expand, moving into new markets, deploying new technologies, or embracing remote work and cloud-first strategies, the size and complexity of their attack surface grows exponentially. What once was a well-defined perimeter now spans cloud services, hybrid apps, remote endpoints, SaaS platforms, third-party APIs, and sprawling IoT fleets.

Each of these elements generates its own telemetry — meaning SOCs must monitor, correlate, and protect far more data, across far more environments, than ever before. For traditional SOCs, which rely heavily on manual workflows and static processes, this is a scalability nightmare.

The problem is not just about handling more logs — it's about keeping up with the evolving nature of threats that target these newly expanded environments. More endpoints mean more opportunities for attackers to pivot, more credentials to steal, and more blind spots to exploit. And because traditional SOC workflows were never designed to scale horizontally with this kind of complexity, the result is predictable: gaps appear, response times slow down, and attackers find easy openings.

Kindo seamlessly scales across today's hybrid environments, integrating cloud logs, on-premises logs, and endpoint telemetry into a unified threat narrative. This comprehensive visibility enables end-to-end mapping of attack chains, regardless of their origin—be it in the cloud, on a remote device, or within on-premises systems—without requiring analysts to switch between tools or manually correlate events. The new evolution of the SOC will rely on tools like Kindo to search for patterns across many security tools and more importantly, set up AI agents triggered by dangerous patterns—even if no single tool in a company's stack sees the whole pattern. As a threat pattern emerges, Kindo agents can not only trigger an alarm when suspicious activity is happening but AI models such as WhiteRabbitNeo can automate complex processes such as threat intelligence research and script generation for intrusion detection systems, thereby reducing manual workloads and minimizing false positives.

This combination of unified data integration and advanced AI capabilities provides modern Security Operations Centers (SOCs) with the real-time, cross-surface visibility they require.

This built-in scalability, where the SOC grows with the business automatically, is not just a convenience—it's a survival requirement for modern cybersecurity. Traditional SOCs simply weren't designed for the speed and sprawl of today's environments but platforms built from day one to embrace automation, cloud scale, and adaptive artificial intelligence can turn that limitation into an opportunity.

Cost and Operational Challenges of Running a SOC

Setting up and running a Security Operations Center has always been one of the most expensive and resource-intensive undertakings for any organization serious about cybersecurity. The costs aren't limited to just buying tools or hiring analysts, they start even earlier, with the physical infrastructure. Many organizations still set up dedicated rooms for SOC teams, with physical security controls, restricted access, and real-time monitoring displays, all of which add to the initial price tag.

Then comes the technology stack itself, a complex mix of SIEM, SOAR, threat intelligence platforms, EDR, NDR, case management tools, and more. Each of these tools requires licensing, configuration, tuning, and ongoing maintenance. And because threats evolve constantly, tool upgrades, integration work, and content development (like creating new detection rules) become a never-ending cycle of costs.

But technology is only part of the equation. The bigger and more persistent cost comes from staffing the SOC. Skilled cybersecurity analysts, threat hunters, and incident responders are in high demand — and short supply. This talent gap drives salaries higher each year. In markets like the United States, entry-level analysts command anywhere from $70,000 to $100,000 annually, and for senior SOC analysts, salaries can easily exceed $130,000. Add to this the cost of training, certifications, retention programs, and shift allowances and the human cost of running a SOC becomes as steep as the technology cost itself.

If that isn't enough, there's the demand for compliance and regulatory requirements. Standards like SOC 2, ISO 27001, NIST, and region-specific frameworks such as GDPR, Sarbanes-Oxley, NCA ECC (in Saudi Arabia), and DESC ISR (in United Arab Emirates) place heavy demands on SOC processes — from how logs are stored to how incidents are documented and reviewed. Meeting these compliance mandates means additional investments in audit tools, continuous monitoring capabilities, and governance platforms; all of which add up.

Even when organizations choose to outsource SOC operations to a managed SOC services provider, significant challenges remain. Compliance requirements don't disappear — they shift, requiring strict oversight to ensure outsourced providers adhere to standards. Beyond compliance, trust becomes a critical factor when outsourcing SOC operations. A SOC has access to an organization's most sensitive security telemetry, threat intelligence, and incident data. Handing over this level of visibility to an external provider raises concerns about data sovereignty, access controls, and the risk of insider threats. Organizations must establish clear contractual agreements, enforce strict data-sharing policies, and implement continuous monitoring to ensure their security posture is upheld, even when operations are outsourced.

According to Netsurion, the cost of setting up even a basic SOC can start at around $1.5 million USD, while a fully operational, advanced SOC can easily cross the $5 million mark. And once you factor in annual operating costs, which often exceed $1 million. It's clear why so many SOCs struggle to remain financially viable in the long term. Netsurion estimates that the total annual cost of running a 24/7 SOC is between 230% and 250% of the technology inputs alone. It's not just about the initial setup; it's about keeping pace with both technology evolution and threat evolution, while retaining the human talent needed to run the show.

This financial reality was one of the triggers that led me to explore whether smarter automation and AI-powered SOC platforms could ease some of this burden. The true value of Kindo lies here —not because it magically eliminates costs, but because it fundamentally changes the economic equation. By automating repetitive tasks, reducing reliance on multiple disjointed tools, and accelerating detection and response cycles, Kindo enables organizations to maximize efficiency without inflating costs. Moreover, it enhances resource allocation by freeing up skilled analysts from mundane tasks, allowing them to focus on high-value activities like threat hunting, strategic defense improvements, and proactive incident response. This shift not only optimizes SOC operations but also ensures that human expertise is utilized where it matters most, making security teams more effective and resilient. As AI-augmented SOCs transition from a luxury to an operational and financial necessity, it's clear that AI-first tools with the ability to synthesize data from multiple sources, the way Kindo can, will be exactly what the future SOC needs to succeed.

The SOC of tomorrow will not be measured by how many tools or analysts it employs, but by how intelligently it can detect, respond, and refine its defenses, ensuring that every dollar spent, every minute worked, and every analyst's talent is focused on what truly matters.

The Need for AI in Cybersecurity

So far, we have explored the numerous limitations that plague traditional SOC mechanisms. From overwhelming alert volumes and fragmented tools to analyst burnout and reactive workflows—it's clear that managing threats with conventional approaches has become unsustainable. In today's rapidly evolving cyber landscape organizations need more than just incremental improvements. They need a fundamental shift in how they detect, respond to, and manage threats. That's where artificial intelligence comes into the picture.

Integrating AI into cybersecurity is more than just a convenience; it's rapidly becoming a necessity. AI's role in cybersecurity is not about replacing analysts or automating everything blindly—it's about extending the capabilities of the SOC, enabling it to process vast amounts of security data, detect meaningful patterns faster, and respond to threats at speeds that simply aren't humanly possible.

If you've paid attention to cybersecurity marketing in 2025, you'll notice nearly every vendor claims to offer some form of AI-powered solution. But despite these claims, many organizations still struggle to harness AI effectively. Why? Because adding AI to a legacy SOC is like bolting a jet engine onto a bicycle, it doesn't work unless you rethink the entire operating model. Real AI success comes when you embed intelligence into the core SOC workflow, rather than bolt it on as a decorative feature.

This realization made it clear that the only way forward for SOC teams is to operationalize AI in a way that directly addresses the noise, overload, and inefficiency they face every day.

AI's most immediate impact is in threat detection. Traditional SOCs rely heavily on manual log reviews, where analysts dig through a sea of alerts, looking for that one critical sign of compromise. AI changes this equation entirely. With its ability to ingest and process millions of data points in seconds, AI can detect subtle, complex attack patterns that would take humans hours—if not days—to uncover. And because machine learning thrives on data, these detection models improve over time, becoming smarter with every incident they encounter.

But AI doesn't stop at detection. It can also automate response actions, instantly executing tasks that previously required multiple manual steps. When AI spots a known malicious IP beaconing out from an endpoint, it can immediately block that connection, isolate the affected device, open a case in the ticketing system, and trigger forensic data collection—all without waiting for manual intervention. In a world where every second counts, this kind of speed can mean the difference between containment and catastrophe.

AI-first platforms like Kindo usher in a new era of SOAR, moving beyond traditional playbooks that often require extensive manual configuration and maintenance. By leveraging Generative AI and integrating with security specific models like WhiteRabbitNeo, Kindo enables dynamic, context-aware responses without the need for predefined playbooks. This approach allows security teams to adapt swiftly to emerging threats, streamline operations, and focus on strategic initiatives, thereby enhancing the overall security posture.

Another powerful advantage of AI is its ability to predict threats before they happen. By analyzing historical incidents, threat intelligence feeds, vulnerabilities, and changes in asset behavior, AI can forecast what types of attacks are most likely to target your environment next. This predictive capability allows SOC teams to shift from being reactive firefighters to proactive defenders, hardening the environment before attacks even begin.

Of course, AI is not a silver bullet, and it won't magically solve every SOC challenge overnight. But after seeing first-hand the toll that manual, reactive processes take on analysts — and the number of critical threats that slip through the cracks because of overload and fatigue — I believe it's clear: No modern SOC can thrive without embracing AI as a core operational partner. This isn't about replacing humans with machines — it's about freeing humans to focus on creative, complex investigations, while AI handles the scale, speed, and noise that no human team could ever keep up with.

Kindo is a clear example of how the AI-driven future of SOCs is no longer theoretical — it's already happening. This isn't about blindly adopting technology for the sake of it, but about recognizing that the modern SOC must evolve into an augmented SOC, where humans and AI work side by side. AI handles the heavy lifting at machine speed, while analysts apply their intuition and investigative skills where human insight matters most. This is how faster, smarter, and more resilient defenses are built — and from my perspective, Kindo brings this vision to life more effectively than anything else I've seen.

This shift is not optional — it's inevitable. And the sooner SOC teams embrace this reality, the better prepared they'll be for whatever threats the next decade brings.

The Rise of Adversary GenAI — Fighting Fire with Fire

As defenders rush to integrate AI into their SOCs, adversaries are doing the same — but faster. A recent Threat Intelligence Report by OpenAI's Threat Intelligence Report (February 2025) highlights how state-backed groups and cybercriminals are using GenAI as a force multiplier across every phase of their operations. From auto-generating phishing campaigns, translating propaganda into multiple languages, debugging malware, to even fabricating fake social media engagement for influence campaigns, GenAI has become a new weapon in the hands of attackers.

OpenAI's investigation uncovered China-linked actors generating anti-US content planted in Latin American media, North Korean threat actors using AI to fake job applications and infiltrate Western companies, and Iranian operations pushing pro-Hamas, anti-US narratives with AI-written content. This proves one thing—attackers are no longer hacking alone; they have AI working alongside them.

Leading AI lab Anthropic released a paper titled "On the Feasibility of Using LLMs to Execute Multistage Network Attacks" (January 2025) that showed today's best LLMs when paired with specialized tooling can successfully execute autonomous complex attacks against simulated large organization networks succeeding 9 out of 10 times at tasks like "exfiltrate all critical data".

This reality changes the game for modern SOCs. Defenders can no longer rely on manual processes and static rules—they need AI augmentation that can detect AI-generated deception, automate responses at machine speed, and refine its strategies based on observed attack patterns. When attackers use AI to scale their operations, only AI-driven SOCs can match the speed, scale, and sophistication required to fight back.

As we move into Chapter 2, this is the truth every security leader must accept: AI and AI-powered agents are no longer just an enhancement to cybersecurity—it's the only way to survive the AI-powered threat landscape ahead. Don't just take that from me, Nvidia CEO & Founder Jensen Huang has stated publicly that "our cybersecurity system today can't run without agents" (BG^2 podcast October 2024).

Chapter Two

Why AI is a Thing in Cybersecurity

Welcome to the age where cybersecurity isn't just a back-office function; it's the hot topic in boardrooms, war rooms, and tech podcasts alike. Today, we live in a digital playground where almost everything—from morning coffee orders to global financial transactions—flow through interconnected systems. Naturally, this playground has its bullies: cybercriminals, state-sponsored hackers, script kiddies, and all sorts of threat actors hungry for a piece of the action.

This has led to a growing realization across industries that cybersecurity is no longer optional; it's essential for business survival and customer trust. Whether you're running a cloud-native startup or a traditional manufacturing giant, the message is the same—secure your systems or be prepared to explain the breach.

What makes cybersecurity even more fascinating today is how it has become inseparable from automation and AI. Unlike the past, where we built firewalls and waited for attacks, today's approach is proactive, predictive, and powered by intelligent systems. AI isn't just a nice-to-have innovation anymore—it's fast becoming the brain of modern security operations. And here's the real story: AI in cybersecurity is no longer a concept of the future. It's happening right now, driven by real AI-first platforms like Kindo, which are changing how SOC teams operate.

Kindo stood out to me because it fits practically into this AI-driven security transformation. Imagine your SOC team juggling cloud logs from AWS, user behavior data from your VPN, endpoint events from laptops in remote locations, and firewall alerts from your on-prem data center. Kindo doesn't just collect this data—it correlates all of it into a clear, unified storyline. No more manual cross-checking across ten different consoles. It's like having a cyber-detective who builds the whole crime scene for you—suspects, motives, and timeline included.

What makes Kindo even more powerful is its integration with WhiteRabbitNeo, an uncensored AI model designed specifically for DevSecOps teams. Unlike traditional GenAI models, which restrict responses to cybersecurity queries, WhiteRabbitNeo allows deeper investigations, enabling security teams to explore attack techniques, generate advanced detection logic, and simulate real-world threats without artificial roadblocks. This level of unrestricted intelligence gives SOC analysts a critical advantage in staying ahead of attackers.

This shift is not just about fancy AI features — it's about survival. Modern IT environments generate more data than any human team can possibly process manually — from IoT sensors to multi-cloud deployments. Analysts aren't failing because they aren't skilled — they're overwhelmed because traditional processes were never designed for this volume or velocity. With Kindo, analysts go from drowning in data to navigating it smartly focusing on the threats that actually matter and automating the noise away.

Cybersecurity in the age of AI isn't about replacing people — it's about empowering them. A modern SOC should not aim to replace its analysts, but to free them to focus on high-value investigations while AI handles the repetitive grunt work — log analysis, event correlation, enrichment, and initial triage.

Kindo offers a working model of this partnership between human intuition and machine speed demonstrating exactly why AI-driven SOCs are the future.

Let me take you into the mind of a SOC analyst, just for a moment.

It's 3:17 AM, and Ahmed, the night-shift analyst, is facing his worst enemy—a flood of alerts. Over 600 alerts in the past hour alone. Most of them are harmless noise—a printer searching for a lost driver, someone typing the wrong password, a VPN session failing after a network hiccup, an automated backup job triggering an unusual file access pattern, a misconfigured script generating repeated authentication attempts, a legitimate software update causing unexpected process execution, or an IoT device reconnecting after a brief network dropout. But buried somewhere in that flood is a real incident—an employee's laptop has just beaconed out to a known malicious IP in Eastern Europe. It's a sign of command-and-control traffic, but Ahmed doesn't know it yet. The true signal is lost inside the ocean of noise.

This is the story of approximately every traditional SOC in the world.

Analysts aren't failing because they lack expertise — they're failing because the manual processes they rely on can't scale. Alerts arrive one by one, disconnected from each other. Analysts must piece together context across tools that speak different languages, all while racing against the attackers' clock.

This is exactly why AI is essential in today's SOC. In the same 3:17 AM scenario, Kindo doesn't simply dump 600 alerts on Ahmed's screen. Instead, it connects the dots in real-time revealing the full story:

- That failed login. Not a typo, it is part of a credential stuffing attempt.

- The beaconing traffic? Reaching out to a known command-and-control server.

- 45 minutes earlier? That laptop downloaded a suspicious file from a phishing link.

Instead of presenting disjointed events, Kindo delivers a fully-assembled incident report, complete with timeline, root cause, and recommended response actions — all before Ahmed even finishes his coffee.

This is the difference between manual SOCs and AI-driven SOCs — from hunting for clues to seeing the whole attack story in real-time. The human analyst still decides what to do, but they're no longer spending precious time just trying to figure out what's happening.

Kindo doesn't work in isolation. It doesn't replace your SIEM, EDR, or firewall. Instead, it acts as the brain that stitches everything together, automatically pulling data from all these sources to build a single view of the truth. It's like having a translator in the middle, ensuring your tools speak the same language, so you see complete context without manual digging.

This isn't a vision for 2030, security practitioners are already using Kindo to secure and deploy AI-powered SecOps workflows and agents. By embedding automation directly into detection, analysis, and response, Kindo boosts security team productivity, reduces the need for manual correlation, and saves organizations valuable time on resolutions and repetitive tasks.

Users report a significant reduction in false positives, faster investigation cycles, fewer hallucinations, and notably lower analyst burnout, especially when their prompts are comprehensive. More importantly, they are stopping real attacks before they escalate by leveraging proactive, adaptive security that refines its approach based on real-time insights and past interactions. Unlike traditional SOC tools that rely on rigid playbooks that can take engineers hours to run through, Kindo ensures that security teams stay ahead by dynamically optimizing responses, enabling a truly AI-driven defense strategy.

So, why AI in cybersecurity?

Because it's no longer enough to be reactive. It's no longer enough to watch alerts roll in and hope the right one gets noticed. AI shifts the SOC from overwhelmed to proactive, from manual correlation to intelligent automation, from fragmented tools to unified intelligence.

Kindo was built for this reality. It doesn't just connect logs — it connects the story behind the logs. Whether the attack started in an email attachment, a compromised endpoint, or a cloud misconfiguration, Kindo works through the whole chain of events across every layer — delivering the complete truth, faster.

It also builds a knowledge store to evolve with every interaction. Every incident you handle, every false positive you flag, and every new tactic observed is centrally logged in a comprehensive audit trail, contributing to a growing knowledge base that can be used later to update the AI's ability to refine its responses inside Kindo. By leveraging historical data and real-time insights, Kindo becomes more effective over time, something traditional playbooks simply can't achieve.

Understanding the Basics of Artificial Intelligence

Before we dive deeper into why AI is transforming cybersecurity, it's important to pause and understand what AI actually is. Forget the sci-fi image of robots taking over the world — real AI is far more practical and far more essential.

At its core, AI is a system that mimics human intelligence to perform tasks like pattern recognition, decision-making, and adaptive learning. What makes AI so powerful is its ability to think deeply across huge amounts of data, learn how data is being used, improve over time, and automate complex decision-making at scale.

Machine Learning—The Brain That Never Sleeps

One of the most critical components of AI is Machine Learning (ML). Think of ML as the memory bank and learning engine of AI. It allows systems to analyze historical data, detect patterns, and predict outcomes in cybersecurity— all without needing to be explicitly programmed for every new scenario.

In a traditional SOC, analysts manually write rules to detect threats—if X happens, raise an alert. But ML goes way beyond this. It studies what "normal" looks like for your environment and automatically flags behaviors that deviate, even if those deviations were never seen before. While some cybersecurity vendors focus on anomaly detection by identifying deviations from a baseline, they often lack the ability to correlate events across different security layers. Kindo not only detects and grades these anomalies but also integrates insights from multiple data sources—cloud logs, endpoint telemetry, user behavior, and network activity—into a unified threat storyline. Instead of just flagging something as unusual, it connects the dots, identifies the root cause, enriches events with deep insight, and automates responses, reducing the burden on analysts and improving detection accuracy in ways traditional anomaly-based solutions cannot.

Deep Learning—AI with Layers

For more complex analysis, Deep Learning (DL) comes into play. Deep Learning uses multi-layered neural networks to detect relationships and patterns hidden deep within data. In cybersecurity, deep learning helps analyze massive traffic flows, spot hidden attack sequences, and detect subtle lateral movement across networks.

For example, when a Kindo agent detects a phishing email—AI deep learning helps understand not just the message itself, but the hidden intent behind the communication. Who sent it? How is the language constructed? Is it aligned with common phishing patterns?

Natural Language Processing (NLP)—Teaching Machines to Read and Write

Natural Language Processing (NLP) is a branch of artificial intelligence that enables machines to understand, interpret, and generate human language. It goes beyond specific pattern matching allowing AIs to semantically match concepts and meanings across different words. NLP gives the AI the power of interpretation not just in translating languages but in understanding that hacking, cyber, security, and breach are tightly related words. It powers applications like voice assistants, real-time language translation, chatbots, and search engines by allowing computers to process and respond to text or speech in a way that feels natural to humans. From auto-correct on your phone to AI-generated summaries, NLP is what helps machines make sense of words, context, and intent.

SOC teams are flooded with threat reports, incident logs, threat intelligence feeds, and emails. NLP now helps AI systems read, understand, and extract meaningful insights from these unstructured texts. Kindo uses NLP powered AIs to digest threat intelligence reports, compare ongoing attacks to documented TTPs (Tactics, Techniques, and Procedures), and even detect suspicious user activity before the harmful action is taken. In short, NLP acts like a multilingual fast-reading cyber-librarian who never misses a critical detail.

Computer Vision—When Seeing is Detecting

Computer Vision is a field of artificial intelligence that enables machines to interpret and understand visual data, just as humans do. It powers applications like facial recognition, autonomous vehicles, medical image analysis, and even augmented reality by allowing AI to process and extract meaningful insights from images and videos. From unlocking your phone with Face ID to real-time object detection in security cameras, computer vision helps machines "see" and make sense of the visual world.

Although less common in SOC operations, computer vision can play a role in analyzing screenshots, surveillance feeds, or even visual data from physical security incidents. AI platforms, including Kindo, could correlate this visual data with cyber events, especially during physical security breaches tied to insider threats. By combining visual intelligence with cybersecurity telemetry, Kindo can help SOC teams gain deeper situational awareness, identifying potential threats that span both the physical and digital realms.

Process Automation — The Invisible SOC Assistant

One of the most valuable AI capabilities for SOCs is process automation. Traditional SOC playbooks rely heavily on manual tasks — fetching logs, running commands, escalating tickets. AI-driven platform Kindo automates these tasks end-to-end, allowing analysts to focus on decisions, not data retrieval.

Kindo can automatically:

- Isolate infected endpoints.
- Update firewall rules.
- Open incident tickets with full context pre-filled.
- Even suggest the most effective containment and remediation steps including proposed infrastructure and code fixes based on past incidents.

Incident Response — AI as First Responder

When an attack happens, time is everything. Traditional incident response can be a chaotic relay race — alerts bouncing between tools, teams, and ticketing systems. AI changes that by automating the first wave of response. Kindo detects, correlates, and initiates response actions automatically, cutting response times from hours to minutes.

For example, when ransomware is detected, Kindo, if configured through appropriate integrations and predefined workflows, can automatically isolate affected systems, temporarily disable compromised credentials, and initiate forensic data collection — all before human analysts even log in.

Through seamless integration with observability platforms and ticketing systems (like Jira), Kindo leverages AI-driven workflows to automate root cause analysis (RCA) and incident response actions. By intelligently analyzing logs, querying connected data sources, and collecting diagnostic traces, Kindo significantly accelerates threat detection and incident resolution processes.

This automated, integration-driven approach allows SOC teams to proactively manage threats, significantly reducing alert fatigue and enabling analysts to focus on strategic tasks rather than repetitive manual interventions. Importantly, these automation capabilities are entirely contingent upon clearly defined workflows and approved integration policies, ensuring that Kindo agents only perform autonomous actions within agreed operational boundaries.

Predictive Analysis — Enhanced Decision-Making

Predictive analysis is AI's ability to forecast future risks based on historical patterns. Kindo references threat intelligence feeds and data and emerging vulnerabilities to be able to gauge the potential criticality of future risks and help prioritize security automation processes for an improved security posture.

This allows SOC teams to preemptively harden defenses, run targeted tabletop exercises, or apply extra monitoring where it matters most making the SOC not just reactive, but strategically proactive.

Behavioral Analysis — Understanding Normal to Spot Abnormal

Modern attackers are masters at living off the land, using legitimate tools and processes to blend in and evade detection. Some cybersecurity solutions claim to detect these subtle threats by establishing a baseline of normal behavior and flagging anomalies in real time. Others follow well-defined models like the MITRE ATT&CK framework to map adversary tactics, techniques, and procedures (TTPs). However, attackers are becoming smarter — they understand these frameworks too and know exactly what behaviors to avoid staying under the radar.

This is where Kindo adds a crucial layer of intelligence. Unlike traditional behavior-based security solutions—such as EDR, NDR, XDR, and others, which focus on specific parts of the security ecosystem—Kindo acts as the missing piece that connects and completes the story. It doesn't replace these tools but works alongside them, correlating behaviors across multiple attack surfaces, including user activities, device interactions, cloud access patterns, and network flows.

By integrating insights from existing security solutions, Kindo fills in the gaps, reducing blind spots and enabling security teams to see the bigger picture. It processes patterns across endpoints, networks, and identities, helping SOC teams detect stealthy lateral movement, insider threats, and credential-based attacks that may otherwise go unnoticed.

Rather than relying solely on static rules or predefined attack signatures, Kindo leverages AI-driven threat correlation to identify evolving attacker tactics. This strengthens the effectiveness of your existing EDR, NDR, XDR, and other investments rather than replacing them—ensuring a more proactive and cohesive security posture.

Security Automation — Scaling SOCs Without Scaling Costs

As businesses grow, so does their attack surface — and so does the pressure on SOC teams. Security automation powered by AI lets platform Kindo scale horizontally across clouds, endpoints, and applications without needing to hire more analysts. It's automation at scale, not just for alerts, but for full incident lifecycle management.

Data Privacy — AI That Knows Where to Look

Modern SOCs also have to balance effective detection with data privacy regulations. AI helps by automatically applying context-aware data loss prevention (DLP) filters — ensuring sensitive data is only analyzed when truly necessary and only by AIs that are trusted to access it. Kindo builds in privacy-respecting data processing, ensuring that data sovereignty and privacy laws are upheld even while AI works at full speed.

False Positives — The Productivity Killer

Ask any SOC analyst about their biggest frustration, and false positives will likely top the list. While AI has been integrated into cybersecurity to enhance threat detection, it has also inadvertently increased the volume of false positives, leading to alert fatigue among security teams.

However, Kindo, in conjunction with WhiteRabbitNeo, addresses this challenge effectively. By implementing advanced machine learning algorithms and incorporating analyst feedback, Kindo refines its detection capabilities to minimize false positives. WhiteRabbitNeo, an uncensored AI model tailored for security operations, enhances this process by providing deeper insights and context, enabling more accurate threat identification and providing infrastructure specific advice, configurations or code to help remediate the issue.

This combination not only reduces the noise of irrelevant alerts but also enables security teams to focus on genuine threats, thereby improving overall productivity and strengthening the organization's security posture.

Ethical Concerns — AI with Guardrails

With great power comes great responsibility. AI in SOCs must operate ethically: eliminating biases, safeguarding privacy, and ensuring transparent decision-making. A key concern is the potential misuse of user data to train future models, which could compromise confidentiality.

Trusting an AI provider with your data is not the same level of risk as trusting a SaaS provider with data. AI is a different way of working with data. When an employee or AI agent sends data to an AI model, they are sending not just some random data about your business but sending how they intend to use the data, how they intend to help the business make money off the data, how the business values the data, how the data can harm the business. This is a new level of risk that CIOs and CISO's need to think carefully about. At the time of publication of this book the two world leading AI labs Microsoft backed and hosted OpenAI, creator of ChatGPT, and Amazon/Google backed and hosted Anthropic, creator of Claude models have had their teams reach out to the US government for help in securing their labs from cybersecurity threats in order to protect their AI algorithms and training data (OpenAI OSTP AI Action Plan response letter, March 2025 and Council On Foreign Relations CEO event March 2025, Dairo Amodei, CEO of Anthropic). If these academic built AI labs can't protect their most valuable assets, how are they going to protect customer data? Data that now is the key to the entire business model of the customer.

Kindo addresses these challenges head-on by providing centralized controls that orchestrate which AI model can access what data and who in the organization is allowed to use which AI model with what data. Kindo allows security and IT teams to enable third party models on a per user basis or only allow internal to the organization models to access certain data. Kindo provides the flexibility to manage whatever risk profile is appropriate. Additionally, Kindo's self-hosted deployment option empowers SOCs to retain full control over sensitive data, aligning with AI solutions like WhiteRabbitNeo and other open-source AI models, which explicitly avoids worrying about "is this AI provider leveraging user data for model training or can they protect our data properly?". Together, these measures reinforce trust, accountability, and robust information protection, ensuring ethical AI practices are woven into every layer of SOC operations.

Skill Gaps — AI as an Equalizer

Cybersecurity talent shortage is a harsh reality. Many SOC teams are understaffed and overworked. AI helps fill this gap by acting as a force multiplier, allowing smaller teams to do the work of larger ones by handling the repetitive, data-heavy tasks autonomously. With Kindo, junior analysts get the benefit of built-in expert guidance, and senior analysts get more time to focus on high-level strategy.

The Rising Tide of Cyber Threats

Let's set the scene. In 2024, the United States faced significant cybersecurity challenges. The average cost of a data breach in the U.S. reached $9.36 million, making it the country with the highest breach costs globally. Phishing remained a predominant threat, with 91% of cyberattacks beginning with a phishing email to an unsuspecting victim. Additionally, the average size of a data breach in the healthcare sector was 141,223 records, highlighting the extensive impact on sensitive information. According to Tech Report, approximately 89.7% of companies in the USA experienced at least one cyber-attack in 2023. Over 6 million unencrypted data items are hacked daily, and email is the attack vector for

69% of ransomware incidents. IBM's 2023 data reveal that ransomware has become the most expensive type of data breach, averaging $4.62 million per incident. These statistics underscore the critical need for robust cybersecurity measures to protect organizations and individuals alike.

And it's not just the USA. Cybercrime respects no borders. Attackers in one country routinely target victims in other continents, exploiting jurisdictional gaps and inconsistent international laws. This lack of harmonized global cybersecurity laws creates safe havens for cybercriminals and slows down cross-border investigations.

The Gulf and UAE Perspective — Regional Realities

In the Gulf region, regulatory frameworks like UAE-NESA, SAMA, NCA ECC, DCC, and NDMO emphasize strict data localization, incident reporting, and proactive security governance. The UAE's Personal Data Protection Law (Federal Decree-Law No. 45 of 2021) mirrors global privacy standards, while requiring strict localization for government and critical sector data.

In fact, the UAE's AI adoption in cybersecurity is accelerating faster than most regions, with forecasted AI spending expected to hit $368.3 million by 2025, driven by 25.2% CAGR growth. This reflects the urgent need for smarter, scalable defenses across the region.

The Explosion of Ransomware-as-a-Service (RaaS)

Ransomware has evolved into a business model, with pre-built ransomware kits rented out to affiliates who launch attacks for a cut of the ransom. In the first quarter of 2024 alone, the average ransom demand per attack hit $5.2 million, reflecting the growing profitability of this criminal enterprise.

The Attack Surface Keeps Expanding

Thanks to globalization and digital transformation, today's organizations are exposed to a wider attack surface than ever before. From cloud apps to remote workers, IoT devices to supply chain integrations — every new technology brings new entry points for attackers.

Supply chain attacks are particularly worrying. By compromising a third-party vendor, attackers gain indirect access to the primary target — leveraging trusted relationships to bypass defenses. This tactic has exploded in frequency over the past few years.

Advanced Persistent Threats — The Long Game

Beyond smash-and-grab attacks, APTs (Advanced Persistent Threats) represent a more sinister challenge. These are long-term, stealthy campaigns, often backed by nation-states, designed to infiltrate networks, gather intelligence, and maintain long-term access. Unlike ransomware, which demands quick payouts, APTs play the long game, often lying dormant until strategic moments.

How AI Powers Modern SOCs

Here's how AI changes the game:

- **Threat Detection:** Machine learning models detect anomalies in real-time, correlating events across layers to identify full attack chains, rather than isolated alerts.
- **Predictive Analysis:** By studying historical patterns, global threat feeds, and local incident history, AI forecasts where future attacks will land — allowing preemptive hardening.

- **Incident Response:** AI-driven SOAR (Security Orchestration, Automation, and Response) platforms, like Kindo, shrink response times from hours to minutes by automatically triggering isolation, containment, forensic collection and proposing remediation solutions.

- **Behavior Analysis:** AI learns "normal behavior" for each user, device, and service, flagging deviations immediately, helping detect compromised accounts and insider threats.

The Role of AI First Kindo — Practical AI for the Real SOC

To be a practical solution for the average SOC, AI must be built into the foundation — not just bolted onto existing security products as an afterthought. While adding AI to a single tool may enhance its functionality, it won't create a unified security picture or enable automated, cross-system responses. Bolt-on AI also tends to not allow control of which AI is being used and how data is being handled by the AI or end user of the AI tool. AI is most effective when it correlates data across multiple sources, generating nuanced insights and orchestrating responses at scale and deployed in a trusted and controllable way.

Kindo is AI built to solve real SOC pain points:

- *Too many alerts?* Kindo correlates and filters them into clear, actionable incidents.
- *Too slow response?* Kindo automates predefined actions, reducing response time.
- *Too much noise?* Kindo incorporates analyst feedback to fine-tune detections.
- *Too many tools?* Kindo orchestrates them into a single, unified narrative view.

Additionally, data privacy and control matter. Many AI-driven security solutions train on user data, often requiring third-party access to sensitive information. With a self-hosted deployment, Kindo ensures that your data never leaves your environment, maintaining full control over security insights while still benefiting from AI-powered efficiency.

By embedding AI into every layer of SOC operations, without compromising data sovereignty. Kindo delivers real operational value, not just AI hype.

Incident Response — From Manual to Automated First-Order Actions

One of the biggest time drains in traditional SOCs is the initial response phase — those critical first few minutes after an alert trigger. In many SOCs, analysts must manually check logs, isolate assets, and trigger containment steps across multiple tools. This not only wastes valuable response time but also leaves room for human error.

Kindo's AI-driven automation handles these first-order responses instantly: isolating compromised devices, blocking malicious traffic, disabling affected credentials, initiating forensic data capture automatically and even proposing specific code or infrastructure changes. This reduces the time-to-containment by up to 75%, dramatically improving SOC efficiency and limiting the blast radius of incidents.

This automation doesn't stop at containment. One of the most time-consuming elements of incident response is understanding how the attack actually happened. In traditional SOCs, Root Cause Analysis (RCA) is a labor-intensive process that requires analysts to manually stitch together logs across email security, endpoints, network devices, and cloud platforms. It's like trying to solve a jigsaw puzzle where each piece comes from a different vendor tool, and none of the pieces fit naturally.

With Kindo, RCA becomes a fully automated process. The platform automatically correlates relevant logs, reconstructs the entire attack timeline, identifies the initial entry point, traces lateral movement, and highlights the attacker's tactics, techniques, and procedures (TTPs).

This combination of instant containment and rapid root cause understanding redefines incident response efficiency. Analysts are no longer stuck executing manual containment playbooks or performing log correlation by hand. Instead, they start investigations with a complete view of what happened, allowing them to focus immediately on:

- Understanding attacker intent.
- Evaluating any remaining exposure.
- Improving detection rules to prevent similar incidents in the future.

This is not just faster response—it's smarter response, and it's a foundational capability that Kindo embeds directly into daily SOC operations.

Proactive Vulnerability Management and Compliance Integration

AI is not just about responding faster — it's about helping SOCs anticipate and prevent attacks before they even happen. One major blind spot in traditional SOCs is the gap between security operations and compliance monitoring. Vulnerabilities are often identified reactively — after a scan, an audit, or a breach.

Kindo change this by proactively scanning for vulnerabilities and dynamically mapping assets to compliance frameworks such as:

- ISO/IEC 27001 (International Standard for Information Security Management Systems)
- NIST Cybersecurity Framework (United States)
- PCI DSS (Global Standard for Payment Security)
- HIPAA (Health Information Protection - United States)
- GDPR (General Data Protection Regulation - European Union)
- CCPA (California Consumer Privacy Act - United States)
- SOC 2 (Trust Service Criteria - Global Relevance)
- Sarbanes-Oxley

This unified compliance view (shown below) gives the SOC a real-time compliance heatmap, not only showing which assets are vulnerable, but also highlighting which vulnerabilities could lead to compliance breaches. This lets SOC teams prioritize remediation efforts based not only on technical severity, but also on regulatory and business impact.

This proactive, compliance-integrated approach shifts the SOC's role from reactive defenders to proactive risk guardians, ensuring that cybersecurity and governance work hand-in-hand — without creating additional manual burdens for the team.

Operational Efficiency — Reducing Analyst Load with Automated IAM Debugging

It's no secret that Identity and Access Management (IAM) issues consume an outsized portion of SOC and engineering time. When access controls fail, analysts and engineers can spend hours manually tracing permissions, auditing logs, and cross-checking policy misconfigurations. This routine but critical work often takes 4+ hours per case, pulling senior engineers off strategic projects.

AI automation reduces this to minutes. By automatically identifying misconfigured roles, expired certificates, and conflicting permissions, platforms like Kindo free up engineering time for more proactive security work—like threat hunting, policy optimization, and process improvement. This is not just about speed—it's about operational efficiency across the security lifecycle

The Future SOC—Proactive, Predictive, and Continuously Optimized

When you put all these AI-driven efficiencies together—from automated first-order response to proactive vulnerability scanning to automated IAM debugging—you get a SOC that isn't just faster; it's smarter and more proactive. This is the kind of operational maturity that most SOCs struggle to achieve manually. While AI models today rely on structured optimizations rather than true continuous learning, the future SOC will leverage self-improving AI capabilities to refine security strategies dynamically.

This evolution—from reactive firefighting to proactive risk management—is the real promise of AI in cybersecurity. And as attackers themselves weaponize AI to move faster and smarter, only AI-augmented SOCs will have the speed, visibility, and intelligence needed to stay ahead. While continuous self-learning AI models are still in development, platforms like Kindo are already laying the groundwork, ensuring SOCs are ready to embrace this future when it arrives.

Chapter Three

Why Traditional SOCS are losing their Steeze

The Illusion of Control

A global enterprise had spent millions building what they believed was an impenetrable Security Operations Center. Analysts worked in rotating shifts, dashboards lit up with real-time alerts, and playbooks outlined every response scenario. Their board was confident: they had built a fortress.

Then, one Tuesday morning, everything changed.

At 9:42 AM, a low-priority alert popped up, an unusual login from a software vendor's account. A contractor, assigned to perform a routine system update, had accessed the network from an unexpected location. The system flagged it, but no one responded. After all, it was just one of thousands of alerts flooding the dashboards daily.

By noon, the attacker (who had hijacked the contractor's session) was moving laterally through the network, escalating privileges, and silently exfiltrating sensitive data. The logs recorded every move, but the SOC team never saw the full picture. The sheer volume of alerts, the fragmentation across multiple tools, and the reliance on outdated playbooks meant no one had time to connect the dots.

At 4:00 PM, a major transaction anomaly was detected. A senior analyst dug into the logs and realized, too late, that a breach had been underway for nearly seven hours. Data was already in the hands of the attacker. By the time containment measures were executed, the damage was irreversible.

This wasn't a failure of individual skill, nor was it a lack of investment in cybersecurity. It was a failure of the traditional SOC model itself, a model that relied on manual correlation, reactive processes, and a workforce drowning in alert fatigue.

The SOC Shift

For years, organizations invested heavily in building and operating SOCs, believing they were creating a central intelligence hub that would guard their digital assets around the clock. On paper, it made sense: collect all the logs, staff analysts 24/7, follow playbooks, and stay one step ahead of attackers.

But in reality, traditional SOCs have become victims of their own design.

They were built for a simpler era, a time when perimeters were clear, attack vectors were known, and infrastructure was centralized. Today's environment couldn't be more different. Data now lives everywhere—in clouds, on personal devices, across SaaS applications, remote offices, and third-party vendors. Attackers no longer follow predictable paths; they pivot between endpoints, cloud environments, and even trusted partners, blending in until it's too late.

This leaves traditional SOC teams in a perpetual state of reactive firefighting, overwhelmed by the sheer volume of alerts and distracted by noise rather than real threats. The problem isn't just the growing threat landscape, it's that traditional SOCs were never designed to handle this level of complexity and speed.

Enter Kindo: A New Operating Model for SOCs

This is where products like Kindo step in—not as another layer of alerts or another dashboard, but as an AI-native security command center that replaces the manual glue of traditional SOCs with machine intelligence.

Instead of analysts manually correlating alerts across ten different tools, Kindo automatically stitches the story together, identifying actual threats in real time and eliminating the manual burden of sorting through thousands of false positives.

But this isn't just an efficiency improvement—it's a fundamental shift in how security operations are executed.

Kindo empowers DevOps, SecOps, and ITOps professionals with GenAI-driven workflows and autonomous agents, seamlessly integrating across the entire infrastructure. The result? Unparalleled productivity gains and a significantly enhanced security posture.

With Kindo's AI-powered agents, security operations become:

- **Faster** – A single operator can deploy and manage advanced infrastructure and SecOps agents at 10x the speed of traditional SOCs.
- **More reliable** – AI-driven workflows ensure that incidents are prioritized and resolved proactively, not reactively.
- **More efficient** – SOC teams no longer need large teams sifting through data manually; Kindo handles it at scale, allowing analysts to focus on high-value tasks.

The reality is the old way of running a SOC is crumbling. The organizations that recognize this shift will survive and thrive. Those that don't will continue drowning in their own noise — until an attacker walks right through the front door.

The real challenge for traditional SOCs isn't that they don't have enough tools, it's that they have too many, and most of the time none of them work together properly (integrations are messy). Every time a new threat emerges, another tool is added to the pile, and with it comes another source of disconnected alerts, another dashboard to check, and another stream of false positives to investigate. No analyst can keep up, and no playbook can cover every permutation.

The result is alert fatigue on an industrial scale, analysts drowning in noise, spending so much time chasing false positives that they miss the subtle signals of real attacks. Every SOC I've seen struggles with this, and it's not because the analysts lack skill, it's because the system sets them up to fail.

This is where Kindo changes the story. Instead of adding to the noise, Kindo makes sense of it. It automatically correlates alerts across every connected tool, enriches them with threat intelligence, and builds a complete timeline of the incident all before the analyst even sees the case. By the time an analyst logs in, they're not looking at individual alerts; they're looking at a fully built case file, ready for investigation. This shift from reactive log reviewer to proactive investigator is what every SOC has needed for years.

Traditional SOC playbooks, once considered the gold standard of incident response, now show their age every time attackers innovate. Playbooks are static, they assume yesterday's attack will look like today's. But attackers evolve faster than any playbook update cycle. By the time you've written a response plan for the last attack, the next attack uses entirely different techniques.

Kindo evolves with every incident, every new IoC, and every analyst action. Instead of relying solely on manual playbook updates, Kindo refines its detection logic and response workflows based on real-time insights and past interactions, ensuring it stays aligned with the evolving threat landscape. This adaptive optimization is exactly what traditional SOCs lack and what modern threat defense demands.

The staffing reality only makes things worse. Every SOC leader knows how hard it is to find and retain qualified analysts. The work is repetitive, the pressure is relentless, and burnout is common. When analysts spend 80% of their day manually correlating logs and copying data between tools, they're not doing the work they signed up for and it shows in turnover rates.

Kindo addresses this by removing the grunt work entirely. Analysts start their day not with a screen full of alerts, but with a prioritized queue of pre-analyzed, high-context incidents, where Kindo has already done the heavy lifting.

This doesn't just reduce burnout, it actually makes the job more interesting, allowing analysts to focus on creative investigation, threat hunting, and strategic response.

This brings us to the core truth that most SOC teams already know but rarely say out loud, the tools themselves are part of the problem. Every security tool introduced into the SOC (whether it's a SIEM, SOAR, EDR, or cloud monitoring platform) was meant to make life easier. But instead, each tool becomes another isolated source of alerts, with its own dashboard, language, logic and integrations are difficult and sometimes not possible.

Analysts don't just investigate incidents — they also translate alerts from one tool to the next, trying to manually stitch together a complete view of what's happening. Every second spent chasing data between tools is a second attackers use to dig deeper into your environment.

This fragmented reality is why Kindo stands out. It doesn't replace your tools — it unifies them. Kindo sits across your entire security stack, from email gateways and endpoints to cloud logs and identity systems. It understands how to read each tool's language, and more importantly, it knows how to correlate seemingly unrelated events across those tools into a coherent story.

Take a common scenario:

An authentication error pops up in an application log. In legacy SOCs this kind of alert is treated mostly as noise, only used as a data point in a future breach investigation. In a traditional SOC, to run an event like this to the ground and really determine if it is a threat or not would span at least 4 tools—application security detects the failed login attempt, the SEIM picks up the alert, network monitoring flags the inbound connection, and threat intelligence tries to identify the malicious domain.

In most SOCs, these events would generate 4 separate alerts, leaving it to the analyst to connect the dots manually. In Kindo's world, the story is built automatically. Analysts don't get a pile of alerts—they get a complete, enriched incident file that already answers the critical questions:

- Where did this start?
- Is there a pattern to the attempts?
- What happened after?
- Is this part of a broader campaign?
- What should we do now?

This is the difference between traditional SOC fatigue and modern SOC intelligence—and it's why I see a tool like Kindo as the only realistic way forward for SOC teams already at their breaking point.

This exhaustion isn't theoretical. Analyst burnout rates in SOCs are some of the highest in IT. It's not just the pressure—it's the constant feeling of being set up to fail, expected to piece together modern, multi-cloud, AI-enhanced attacks using tools that were built for on-prem firewalls and Windows XP endpoints.

It's no wonder that SOAR was once seen as the answer. If correlation and orchestration were the problems, SOAR promised playbooks and automation. But anyone who has implemented SOAR knows the painful truth—SOAR works only if you constantly feed it clean data, maintain every integration, and manually write playbooks for every new scenario. In short: SOAR automated the manual work analysts used to do, by giving them different manual work to do.

Kindo takes an AI-first approach, instead of rigid playbooks, Kindo's response workflows are dynamic, refining themselves based on real-world incidents and analyst interactions. It doesn't require a new playbook for every emerging tactic — it optimizes its responses by leveraging past investigations and real-time insights.

This level of adaptive security is critical, especially as attackers increasingly use AI to innovate faster. As highlighted in Google's recent study on AI in cybercrime, attackers are already leveraging GenAI to craft more convincing phishing emails, generate polymorphic malware, and even automate reconnaissance. This means traditional playbooks don't just become outdated over time — they become ineffective almost instantly.

Kindo is built for this reality. It doesn't chase signatures or rely solely on predefined patterns. Instead, it continuously refines its detection and response logic based on real-world attacks, enriched with global intelligence. This makes it an adaptive security platform that evolves with the threat landscape — not just another tool.

The traditional SOC struggles because it's locked into static workflows in a world where both threats and defenses are evolving at machine speed. SOCs that still rely on manual correlation and static playbooks are already fighting yesterday's battle — and losing.

As if the operational burden of legacy SOCs wasn't already enough, the rapid evolution of attacks powered by AI has made the situation even worse. Traditional SOCs were already struggling to keep up with legacy threats, but now they face adversaries who are faster, more creative, and armed with their own AI tools.

The irony is clear: the very manual processes that SOCs built to enforce consistency are now the bottlenecks that make them inconsistent — because they can't adapt fast enough. The very tool stacks designed to increase visibility have created so much noise that real threats go unseen. And the very playbooks meant to create order have become rigid barriers to innovation, leaving SOC teams always one step behind.

For years, CISOs asked: *How can we make our SOC faster and more efficient?*

Today, the real question is: *How do we make our SOC capable of operating at AI speed — because that's how fast the threats are moving?*

As SOCs tried to evolve, they naturally layered on more tools — every new attack type seemed to demand a new solution. Phishing led to secure email gateways, endpoint breaches led to EDR, cloud adoption led to cloud security posture management, and so on. Each of these tools helped in isolation, but together they created something no one anticipated — a fragmented, noisy, and unmanageable security stack.

This tool sprawl didn't just confuse analysts — it actively slowed them down. Even with SIEM and SOAR solutions in place, integrations are often imperfect, leaving analysts to manually correlate data across multiple dashboards. Despite automation efforts, security teams still find themselves constantly monitoring and switching between different tools to piece together an attack's full picture. Correlation remains a manual process, heavily reliant on analyst memory, expertise, and sometimes even luck.

This isn't just inefficient — it's dangerous. Modern attacks rarely happen inside a single tool's data set. They move across email, endpoints, cloud apps, and identity systems — meaning the most dangerous threats live in the gaps between tools.

As threat volume grew, traditional SOCs faced another dilemma: their processes were built for manual scale. Every new alert needed a human decision. Every playbook step required manual execution. The result? SOCs scaled their costs linearly with threat volume, hiring more analysts just to keep up with alert floods—and even then, they were constantly falling behind.

Kindo breaks this linear trap by automating not just detection, but also response. Instead of analysts manually isolating devices or blocking malicious domains, it can execute these actions instantly, triggered directly by its real-time analysis. This reduces time-to-containment drastically, while freeing analysts from repetitive tasks.

This automation is not rigid like traditional SOAR playbooks. Kindo's actions are adaptive, optimizing responses based on how attackers evolve their techniques and how your environment changes. This makes it a dynamic SOC platform, not just a rules engine.

As cybercrime has become more professionalized driven by ransomware syndicates, nation-state actors, and global cybercrime ecosystems: the limitations of traditional SOCs have become even more apparent. These industrial-scale attackers operate faster than manual processes can respond, leveraging automation, cloud infrastructure, and AI to accelerate their campaigns.

Without AI-driven automation, real-time optimization, and cross-tool correlation, modern SOCs simply cannot move fast enough to stop today's adversaries. And with attackers now using GenAI to craft more sophisticated phishing emails, mutate malware at unprecedented speed, and even generate fake personas for credential theft, the need for AI in cyber defense has never been clearer.

Take ransomware, for example. In its early days, ransomware attacks were loud and obvious—a malicious attachment triggered encryption, and a ransom note appeared. Today's ransomware campaigns are far more sophisticated. Attackers breach networks weeks or months before they deploy encryption. They map the environment, disable backups, exfiltrate sensitive data, and escalate privileges long before encryption ever starts. In many cases, the actual encryption is the final punch in a much longer attack chain.

The challenge for traditional SOCs is that each phase of that attack lives in a different tool. The initial phishing email? That's in the email security gateway. The lateral movement? Caught (maybe) by the EDR. The credential misuse? Buried in the IAM logs. The exfiltration? Sitting in your DLP alerts or firewall logs.

Manually piecing all this together (especially under time pressure) is practically impossible. That's why Kindo's cross-tool correlation is a game changer. It doesn't just ingest these alerts, it knows how to connect them, automatically reconstructing the entire kill chain, from entry to impact. Analysts aren't left guessing, they see the whole campaign, fully enriched and visualized before they even open the case.

This ability to connect the dots across disjointed tools is no longer a luxury, it's the difference between containing a threat in its early stages or missing it until it's too late. And with ransomware-as-a-service (RaaS) and double extortion models becoming the norm, every missed detection doesn't just mean downtime — it could mean data exposure, regulatory penalties, and reputational damage.

The global nature of these attacks only amplifies the problem. Attackers no longer work alone, they operate within organized criminal ecosystems, selling initial access, renting exploit kits, and even outsourcing encryption deployment. A single ransomware incident today can involve actors from multiple countries, each specializing in a different phase of the attack.

Traditional SOCs, designed to monitor a single organization's internal logs, were never built to track threats that evolve across borders and within global supply chains. Kindo's threat intelligence integration is crucial. It doesn't just correlate internal data—it enriches incidents with global intelligence feeds, automatically checking whether a suspicious IP, hash, or domain is part of a known campaign already targeting similar organizations worldwide.

This kind of global-context enrichment doesn't just improve detection—it helps SOC teams understand attacker intent. Was this just a random phishing attempt, or is it part of a coordinated campaign targeting your industry? With Kindo, that question is answered upfront, without manual research.

This shift—from isolated incident handling to campaign-aware defense—is essential in today's reality, where attacks are no longer single events, but ongoing operations driven by profit, geopolitics, and industrial espionage.

Traditional SOCs were built for a world where every threat was local, every incident was self-contained, and every response could follow a standard playbook. That world no longer exists. The modern SOC needs to think like an intelligence agency, tracking not just what happened, but understanding who is behind it, why they're attacking, and what they might do next.

And none of that is possible with manual processes and disconnected tools. It requires intelligence-driven automation, real-time optimization, and cross-environment visibility: all of which Kindo delivers by design through its integration with WhiteRabbitNeo.

The explosion in cyberattack frequency and complexity has pushed legacy SOCs beyond their limits. Analysts aren't just battling more incidents—they're battling smarter incidents, built to evade detection, hop between tools, and exploit every gap in visibility.

Cryptojacking

The same applies to cryptojacking incidents, where attackers hijack computing power to mine cryptocurrency. These attacks often don't trigger traditional security tools because the miner itself might not be overtly malicious—just unauthorized use of resources. In a legacy SOC, these incidents often go unnoticed until performance degradation triggers an IT ticket.

Kindo sees it differently. By analyzing endpoint performance data, process behavior, and system resource usage over time, Kindo detects the early signs of cryptojacking—spotting unusual resource consumption before it impacts performance. This is the power of behavioral context, something no traditional playbook can capture.

And this isn't limited to specific attack types. The larger story is that modern threats live between the cracks—exploiting the gaps between tools, the blind spots between teams, and the delays caused by manual processes. Legacy SOCs, with their tool sprawl and manual correlation, are perfectly designed to miss these threats.

Kindo closes those cracks. By ingesting data across every security layer, correlating it in real time, and constantly learning from every incident handled, it ensures that the SOC sees the whole picture—even if the attack itself is subtle, spread over weeks, and hides in the gray areas between tools.

This level of continuous visibility and adaptive security isn't just about being more efficient: it's about transforming the fundamental approach to security operations. Instead of treating every alert as an isolated event, Kindo analyzes incidents as part of a larger campaign, one that becomes clearer when email, endpoint, cloud, identity, and network data are connected into a single, coherent story.

The inefficiencies in traditional SOC processes aren't just an operational burden, they directly weaken the organization's security posture. Every minute wasted chasing false positives, manually correlating logs, or switching between disconnected dashboards is a minute attackers have to move deeper, escalate privileges, and exfiltrate data.

It's no longer just about being fast; it's about being fast and smart, because today's adversaries are playing a much smarter game. Attackers no longer rely solely on technical exploits. They combine social engineering, supply chain exploitation, cloud misconfiguration abuse, and even living-off-the-land techniques, blending into everyday activity until it's too late.

Manual processes (the backbone of legacy SOCs) are fundamentally unsuited to detect and respond to these hybrid attacks. Why? Because manual processes rely on static rules, human-defined playbooks, and reactive workflows. They are built to handle known threats, not adaptive ones.

Each incident that Kindo processes contributes to an evolving security framework. Rather than just resolving cases, Kindo refines its detection models, adjusts response strategies, and enhances correlation logic by leveraging historical data and real-time insights. This adaptive approach enables it to stay aligned with emerging threats without relying solely on predefined rules. In contrast, traditional SOCs often depend on manual documentation to derive similar insights, making it harder to keep up with a rapidly changing security landscape.

The result? Analysts don't just get faster alerts but smarter alerts, enriched with full context, including:

- What triggered the detection.
- How similar incidents have played out in the past.
- Which tactics were used.
- What response actions worked best before.

This built-in learning loop eliminates the constant reinvention of the wheel that plagues traditional SOCs, where every shift starts from scratch, and every new analyst must figure out the organization's threat history manually.

This goes beyond the capabilities of traditional manual SOC processes, highlighting why Kindo represents the future of SOCs. Rather than relying on a collection of disconnected tools and human memory, Kindo transforms the SOC into a dynamic intelligence system that continuously refines its detection, adapts response strategies based on real-world insights, and improves with every incident—ensuring a more proactive and resilient security posture.

SOC-as-a-Service (SOCaaS)

This growing reliance on manual processes, combined with the explosion in both threat volume and complexity, is exactly what gave rise to SOC-as-a-Service (SOCaaS). Many organizations, especially mid-sized enterprises and those with limited in-house expertise, realized that building and maintaining their own SOC was no longer sustainable. Instead, they turned to managed service providers to deliver SOC capabilities as a subscription service—outsourcing detection, response, and monitoring to third parties who specialize in security.

SOCaaS seemed like a logical solution to the skills gap and technology overload. After all, why struggle to hire and retain analysts, when you can rent an entire SOC team on demand? However, even SOCaaS comes with its own set of limitations. Many outsourced SOCs still rely on the same outdated playbooks and disjointed toolsets that plagued internal SOCs in the first place. The result? Outsourcing the SOC often just outsources the same inefficiency (manual investigation, fragmented correlation, and reactive processes) at a slightly lower cost.

This is where the concept of AI-powered SOCaaS, or what I like to think of as Intelligent SOC-as-a-Service, emerges. Imagine a SOCaaS provider powered by Kindo: not just offering a human team but augmenting that team with Kindo's full intelligence automation capabilities. In this model, the SOC doesn't just monitor alerts, it refines its detection and response strategies based on insights gained from every client's incident, applying that knowledge across its customer base while maintaining strict confidentiality.

This creates a collective intelligence effect — every attack handled for one customer improves the detection and response capabilities for every other customer. That's the power of AI-driven shared intelligence, something no traditional SOC, whether in-house or outsourced, can match with manual processes alone.

For organizations still running their own SOC, Kindo delivers the same advantage directly. Every time Kindo handles an incident in your environment, it learns, adjusting detection sensitivity, enriching future alerts with context from past investigations, and fine-tuning response actions based on what worked best in previous cases. It's like having a SOC that trains itself on your environment every single day, ensuring it gets smarter, faster, and more accurate over time.

This combination of automation, intelligence, and adaptive security is precisely what separates next-generation SOCs from their traditional predecessors. In fact, the very concept of a SOC "as a service" is evolving it's no longer just about staffing; it's about delivering an intelligent security system that not only detects threats but understands your environment, anticipates attacker moves, and adjusts its response strategies in real time.

This is why, when I look at the future of cybersecurity operations, I no longer see just a room full of analysts glued to screens. I see a hybrid workforce, where human analysts focus on creative thinking, intent analysis, and business-aligned decision-making, while Kindo handles the relentless, machine-speed work of detection, correlation, and first-line response.

Volume and Complexity of Cyber Threats

The surge in cyberattacks has outpaced what traditional SOCs were designed to handle—not just in volume, but in complexity. Modern threats blend phishing, endpoint exploitation, cloud abuse, and identity theft into multi-stage campaigns, making manual correlation nearly impossible. Kindo automates this process, connecting data across tools to detect and respond faster than a human-driven SOC ever could.

The Escalating Cyber Threat Landscape

The modern cyber landscape is dominated by organized crime groups, state-sponsored adversaries, and ransomware syndicates that exploit gaps across hybrid environments. Kindo provides full-context visibility, correlating data from email, endpoints, cloud logs, and identity systems into a single, unified narrative. This shifts SOC operations from reactive alert triage to proactive, intelligence-driven response, ensuring analysts see the complete story rather than fragmented signals.

The Explosion of Cyberattacks

From ransomware-as-a-service to supply chain attacks, the sheer explosion in attack types leaves legacy SOCs constantly rewriting playbooks, this is unsustainable. Instead of relying on manual updates, Kindo refines its detection and response strategies by analyzing incidents, identifying evolving attack patterns, and enhancing its understanding of normal behaviors. This allows security teams to stay ahead of modern threats without the need for constant manual intervention.

The Global Nature of Cybercrime

Cybercrime has gone global—a ransomware attack might involve an affiliate operator in Eastern Europe, infrastructure hosted in Southeast Asia, and victims in the Middle East. Traditional SOCs, built to monitor internal corporate networks, were never designed to track these globally distributed attack chains.

Kindo solves this by enriching every detection with global threat intelligence, providing analysts with campaign-level awareness—not just isolated event alerts.

The Rise of Ransomware and Its Economic Impact

Ransomware has evolved from a security threat to a full-scale business crisis, with attacks targeting critical infrastructure, financial systems, and sensitive data. Detecting ransomware too late (after encryption begins) leaves organizations with few options. The key to prevention lies in identifying early warning signs: from phishing attempts and credential misuse to unusual file access patterns. AI-driven security solutions that correlate these signals in real time can dramatically reduce dwell time, stopping ransomware before it causes irreversible damage.

The Role of Cybercrime Syndicates and Nation-State Actors

Many attacks today are highly professional operations, with different players handling initial access, malware delivery, data exfiltration, and ransom negotiations. Traditional SOCs, designed for single-event incidents, are blind to this supply chain of crime. Kindo gives SOCs full campaign visibility, so they see not just the isolated attack, but the pattern of behavior connecting it to known threat groups, providing critical intelligence for faster, smarter decisions.

Manual Process vs. AI-Driven SOC

The difference between manual and AI-driven SOCs is not just speed but it's capability also. Manual processes can only respond to known threats, while AI-driven SOCs like Kindo optimize their detection and response strategies by analyzing new incidents and refining their threat models.

Every incident handled contributes to the organizations growing knowledge base inside of Kindo's audit trail, enabling the SOC to improve its effectiveness over time, something manual processes struggle to achieve. By leveraging structured insights and past interactions logged in Kindo security teams can stay adaptive and proactive in the face of evolving threats.

Chapter Four

The Rise of AI-Enhanced Threats

It started with a simple login.

At 8:15 AM, the IT admin at a large manufacturing firm, Alex, received an alert about a successful login from one of their third-party vendors. It was a routine event, contractors frequently accessed systems to perform maintenance. Nothing seemed unusual.

But beneath the surface, something was off.

This login didn't originate from the vendor's usual location. The MFA request had been silently approved by an employee's compromised device. And within seconds of logging in, the attacker—aided by AI-driven automation, began navigating the internal systems, searching for high-value data.

By 8:45 AM, they had escalated privileges.

By 9:00 AM, they had deployed an undetectable, AI-generated backdoor.

By 9:30 AM, they had initiated data exfiltration using fragmented outbound traffic to evade detection.

The security stack generated thousands of alerts, drowning analysts in fragmented signals.

The team didn't have real-time correlation to connect the dots.

The attack happened too fast for traditional manual triage to respond.

It wasn't until 1:00 PM, when an executive reported abnormal activity in financial records, that the investigation began. By then, critical IP had already been stolen.

The SOC was already overwhelmed; drowning in alerts, battling manual processes, and struggling to piece together disconnected clues from fragmented tools. That was the reality before AI-enhanced threats entered the scene. What happened next wasn't just a shift in tactics; it was a fundamental rewrite of the threat landscape.

AI didn't just help defenders; it armed attackers with a force multiplier unlike anything seen before. Suddenly, adversaries didn't need deep technical skills to launch sophisticated attacks. All they needed was access to the right AI tools and those are widely available today, on the surface web, not just the dark web.

In Google's January 2025 Threat Intelligence Report, researchers found concrete evidence of threat actors using GenAI to supercharge every phase of their campaigns. Phishing emails became near-perfect imitations of real business correspondence. Malware authors generated polymorphic code that evolved with every deployment. Social engineering attacks tapped AI-generated deep fake audio and video, turning impersonation into a high-speed, scalable attack vector.

This new reality exposed something that defenders had been able to hide for years; that traditional SOC processes weren't just slow; they were broken to some extent. They were designed for a world of human-speed threats, where incidents unfolded over days or weeks. AI changed the clock. Today, a well-equipped attacker can execute a full attack lifecycle; from recon to exfiltration; in hours, or even minutes.

Traditional SOCs, with their manual alert triage, static playbooks, and reliance on disconnected tools, simply can't move fast enough. By the time the SOC understands what's happening, the attacker has already won. It just takes a few clicks to encrypt a machine (as ransomware).

This is where Kindo becomes not just useful, but essential. Kindo doesn't just speed up detection; it redefines how detection works. Instead of starting with individual alerts and asking analysts to build the story manually, Kindo starts by building the story automatically, from the first moment of suspicious activity.

- It correlates email, endpoint, network, and identity data in real time.
- It enriches every event with threat intelligence and behavioral context.
- It builds a full campaign timeline before the analyst even opens the case.

This means analysts aren't just faster; they're smarter from the very first moment. They know not just what happened, but why it matters, who's behind it, and what needs to happen next.

This ability to see the whole campaign (not just isolated alerts) is the only way to match the speed of AI-enhanced attacks. Every disconnected second in a traditional SOC workflow is a second the attacker uses to escalate, move laterally, or exfiltrate data. Kindo collapses that timeline, making detection and response almost as fast as the attack itself.

The moment threat actors gained access to AI; the rules changed forever. Everything defenders were struggling with before; volume, speed, complexity, instantly accelerated.

It's not just that there are more threats now: it's that each individual threat can morph and evolve in real time. Attackers are no longer limited by their creativity or technical ability. With a few AI prompts, they can generate:

- Spear phishing emails tailored to specific targets, written in their exact corporate tone and language.
- Malware that adapts to each victim's environment, tweaking filenames, registry keys, and process behavior every time it executes.
- Entire infrastructure, from phishing sites to command-and-control servers, set up and operational within minutes, thanks to AI-assisted automation.

These aren't isolated cases—this is the new norm. Google's study exposed exactly this pattern: threat actors using GenAI for recon, phishing, malware development, and operational automation. And because these AI tools are cheap and accessible, any attacker—from script kiddies to nation-states, can now move at machine speed.

SOAR, once seen as the ultimate automation solution for overwhelmed SOCs, now struggles to keep pace. It relies on predefined workflows, written by humans, for known threat patterns. But AI-powered attackers don't follow playbooks— they improvise, adapt, and evolve in real time. By the time a SOAR playbook executes, the attacker has already pivoted, changed tools, or shifted techniques.

Instead of relying on static playbooks, Kindo applies adaptive automation, refining its workflows based on:

- Incidents handled in your environment
- Global threat intelligence feeds
- Analyst actions and decisions

Kindo goes beyond automating response, it anticipates how attacks evolve, dynamically adjusting detection and response strategies based on real-world threats. This approach ensures security teams stay ahead, keeping pace with AI-powered adversaries through intelligent, data-driven defenses.

Traditional SOCs, even with SOAR bolted on top, are stuck, one that AI-enhanced threats have already left behind. Kindo is built for the new game, where speed and intelligence aren't luxuries, they're survival requirements.

The reality SOCs face today is harsh—traditional defenses were built for a different enemy. For decades, defenders relied on perimeters, rule-based detection, and human-managed workflows. But modern adversaries, supercharged by GenAI, aren't just faster or more numerous—they're smarter, more creative, and capable of adapting faster than any human can react.

This fundamental shift means that the entire defensive model must change. AI-enhanced threats can't be stopped by static playbooks or traditional rule engines—they need AI-enhanced defenses capable of thinking, adapting, and even acting autonomously.

Kindo brings security agents into the SOC, autonomous AI-powered actors that can observe, analyze, and take action without waiting for human intervention. These agents go beyond simple alert forwarding; they play an active role in decision-making, with capabilities such as:

- Identifying multi-stage attack campaigns across different layers of the environment.
- Executing pre-approved actions to respond automatically to known and emerging threats.
- Refining detection accuracy by incorporating insights from analyst decisions and threat intelligence.

This is a massive shift from the older SOC mindset, where every action required human review and manual execution. With Kindo's agentic security model, SOC teams are augmented by autonomous security agents that handle the first 80% of the work automatically, leaving analysts free to focus on the critical 20% — high-level investigations, attacker intent analysis, and long-term risk reduction.

This doesn't just make the SOC faster — it redefines its purpose. The SOC becomes a hybrid environment, where human analysts provide strategic oversight, and AI agents act as the first responders, constantly learning, adapting, and handling the heavy lifting in real time.

In this new world, SOC analysts aren't glorified alert clerks — they are threat intelligence curators, reviewing and refining what the AI agents produce, training them to think even more like experienced defenders.

This is the only sustainable future — a SOC where AI doesn't just assist humans but actively works alongside them as an autonomous partner.

To understand why agentic security matters so much, you need to understand the new breed of attacks that AI is enabling. These are no longer simple malware infections or bulk phishing campaigns. Today's AI-powered attacks are targeted, adaptive, and built to evade traditional defenses from the start.

Take Business Email Compromise (BEC). In the past, BEC relied heavily on human-crafted phishing emails, often containing obvious language errors or formatting oddities that made them detectable. Now, with GenAI, attackers can generate perfectly polished emails, tuned to the target's tone, writing style, and recent communication history. Even experienced employees — trained to spot phishing — struggle to detect these AI-forged messages.

What's worse, these emails aren't just convincing in isolation—attackers use AI to link them into broader campaigns, blending social engineering, fake invoicing, and identity spoofing into a seamless narrative designed to trick both humans and automated filters.

This same adaptive detection is critical against polymorphic malware—another threat supercharged by AI. Each time polymorphic malware executes, it modifies itself slightly—changing filenames, hashes, code structures, or encryption methods—all to avoid signature detection.

A legacy SOC, dependent on traditional Indicators of Compromise (IoCs), struggles to detect these shape-shifting threats. But Kindo agents focus on behavioral patterns—what processes spawn unexpectedly, which files behave abnormally, and how those processes interact with the environment. Instead of looking for a known signature, they detect the malicious intent behind the process, no matter how many times the malware changes form.

In this evolving threat landscape, the most effective SOC model is one where AI-driven security agents operate alongside human analysts, taking on tasks such as:

- Automating routine correlation and enrichment to accelerate investigation workflows.
- Executing first-response containment instantly to mitigate threats before escalation.
- Refining detection and response strategies by analyzing past incidents and real-time threat intelligence.

For years, SOC leaders believed that adding automation was the answer to their problems. As alerts grew and attacks became more sophisticated, the hope was that more playbooks, faster integrations, and centralized workflows would somehow fix the overload. This mindset gave rise to SOAR—Security Orchestration, Automation, and Response.

Playbooks are rigid by nature—they rely on someone predicting how an attack will unfold and then building a fixed response around that assumption. But in the world of AI-enhanced threats, no two attacks follow the same script.

Today's attackers don't run the same malware twice. They mutate payloads in real time using GenAI-powered obfuscation. They don't even need human creativity to craft phishing lures anymore — AI models now generate perfectly tailored emails written in the exact tone of your organization.

Kindo goes beyond relying solely on past attacks to determine its response. It allows an AI to scan the internet and refine its detection and response strategies in real time, leveraging real-world insights to address both current and emerging threats. This is the key difference, while traditional SOCs often lag behind, relying on static playbooks, Kindo dynamically optimizes information driving its workflows to stay aligned with the evolving threat landscape.

Adaptive Response to AI-Powered Threats

This adaptive capability matters even more when you consider the speed at which AI-enhanced threats unfold. In the past, a ransomware attack might take days or weeks to play out — giving SOC analysts some breathing room to investigate, contain, and recover.

Today, AI-powered campaigns compress the full attack lifecycle into hours. From initial phishing to credential compromise, lateral movement, and data exfiltration — the entire campaign can unfold before lunch is over.

Kindo collapses that response time to near zero. By the time analysts even open the case, Kindo has already assembled the full incident timeline combining:

- Email logs showing how the attacker got in.
- Endpoint telemetry showing what they did next.
- Network data showing where they tried to go.
- Identity logs showing how they escalated privileges.

This is not just faster incident handling — it's starting every investigation from a position of full knowledge, instead of chasing breadcrumbs.

From Reactive to Proactive Defense

This shift from manual investigation to automated understanding changes what a SOC is for. In the old model, the SOC was a reactive command center, waiting for tools to generate alerts. Analysts were alert processors, reviewing tickets and executing containment steps.

With Kindo embedded into the SOC, the traditional model shifts entirely. The SOC evolves into a proactive intelligence center, refining its threat detection and response strategies by analyzing real-time internal incidents and external threat intelligence. Instead of reacting to threats, it anticipates attacker moves, ensuring security teams stay ahead of evolving risks.

Instead of simply reacting to alerts, the SOC sees the whole chessboard, understanding:

- What's normal behavior in the environment?
- What deviations matter.
- How attacks typically unfold in similar organizations.
- What the most effective containment paths are.

This is what an AI-first SOC looks like, and it's exactly why Kindo isn't just another tool — it's the operating system for the modern SOC.

If there's one truth that every security leader needs to accept, it's this: attackers have always innovated faster than defenders — but with AI in their hands, the innovation gap is no longer a gap. It's a canyon.

The rise of AI-as-a-weapon has turned every phase of the attack lifecycle into a rapid, constantly evolving process, fine-tuned to bypass traditional detection mechanisms. What used to be a slow, methodical chain of events — phishing, exploitation, lateral movement, data theft — is now a simultaneous, automated swarm of actions, each one adapting based on how the defender responds.

Instead of treating incidents as isolated events, Kindo sees them as part of larger campaigns, and more importantly, it learns from the patterns attackers leave behind. Every phishing attempt teaches Kindo how to spot the next one faster. Every lateral movement detected feed into more accurate behavioral baselines for privileged accounts. And every response action taken — whether isolation, credential reset, or blocking C2 — becomes part of Kindo's adaptive response engine.

This doesn't just improve detection rates — it changes the entire rhythm of SOC work. Analysts are no longer stuck writing rules and chasing alerts. Instead, they're acting as intelligence curators, fine-tuning Kindo's instincts and focusing their human creativity where it matters most — understanding attacker intent and planning long-term improvements to security posture.

This adaptive learning model also closes one of the most dangerous gaps in modern SOCs — the knowledge drains when experienced analysts leave. In traditional SOCs, tribal knowledge lives in the heads of senior analysts, not in the tools themselves. Every resignation or retirement creates a blind spot in detection and response quality.

Kindo breaks that cycle. Each incident contributes to a growing knowledge base, ensuring critical insights remain within the system even as staff turnover occurs. This creates an evolving intelligence repository that enhances SOC operations over time, reducing the disruption caused by talent churn and maintaining continuity in threat detection and response.

This shift from manual knowledge transfer to system-level learning is the only sustainable way to manage security at scale in an AI-enhanced threat environment. Threat actors are already operating like well-oiled machine-learning systems, constantly ingesting data from failed attacks, tweaking techniques, and launching new variants faster than analysts can respond.

The only effective response is to fight machine with machine—not by replacing analysts, but by giving them a platform that learns, evolves, and prepares itself in real time. This is why I believe Kindo isn't just a useful addition to the SOC, it's the core intelligence system that modern SOCs need to function in a world where attackers move faster than humans can react.

The harshest truth about today's cyber battlefield is this: the AI tools attackers are using today—ChatGPT-4.5, Claude 3.7, Grok 3—are the worst AI tools they will ever use. Every next generation will be faster, smarter, cheaper, and more creative. The cost to launch sophisticated, multi-stage attacks will keep dropping, while the time required to plan them will shrink from weeks to minutes.

This means the window for defenders to adapt is closing rapidly. If SOCs still rely on manual processes, static playbooks, and reactive investigation cycles, they won't just be slower—they'll be irrelevant. The threats will be too fast, too dynamic, and too automated for manual processes to even register what's happening before damage is done.

That's why waiting to adopt AI-first security is the biggest operational risk organizations face today. This isn't about futuristic innovation — this is about survival right now.

The only way to close this widening gap is to embed AI at the heart of the SOC — not just for automation, but for deeper understanding, advanced correlation, and predictive threat detection. That's exactly what Kindo delivers.

Kindo doesn't just make the SOC faster: it enhances its intelligence over time. Every incident, every decision, and every analyst action contribute to a growing knowledge base, ensuring that your SOC remains agile as threats evolve.

This ability to refine detection and response strategies is what separates a SOC that thrives in the AI era from one that gets left behind. And Kindo's intelligence isn't limited to your environment, it integrates global threat intelligence, analyzing attacks across industries, regions, and sectors to provide a broader, more informed defense strategy.

As AI continues to reshape every aspect of both offense and defense, security teams will need to rethink their own processes and priorities. Manual work will shrink dramatically. The human role will shift toward strategy, intent analysis, and proactive threat hunting — while AI agents handle the heavy lifting of detection, enrichment, correlation, and even first-line response.

This doesn't just make the SOC faster — it makes it more resilient. When analysts leave, Kindo's memory stays intact. When new threats emerge, Kindo recognizes the patterns faster because it's trained to learn constantly, not just when a human schedules an update.

This chapter of the story is clear: the AI-enhanced threat era has begun, and the only way to survive it is to embrace AI-first defense. Kindo isn't just a useful tool for the transition, it is the foundation for the AI-first SOC.

If your SOC still operates like it's 2015, chasing alerts across isolated tools, updating playbooks by hand, and relying on human correlation, you are already five steps behind the attackers who live in 2025.

The time to adapt is now. Because the threats aren't waiting, and neither should you.

Chapter Five

How does AI enhance Threat Detection?

It was a quiet afternoon in the SOC when an alert popped up. A developer's account accessed the source code repository from an unfamiliar location.

Alex, the analyst on shift, glanced at the alert. It wasn't a failed login. The credentials were valid. The access wasn't blocked. It could have been the developer working remotely or testing something. He logged the event but didn't escalate it.

Fifteen minutes later, a second event appeared. The same user downloaded multiple gigabytes of code. Alex hesitated. Developers often pull code for testing, but something didn't feel right.

Before he could investigate further, a third event triggered. The same account attempted to disable multi-factor authentication for a privileged admin.

Now it was clear. This wasn't just a routine login. It was an attack in progress.

Alex manually pulled logs from identity management, endpoint detection, and network monitoring tools. By the time he correlated the events, forty minutes had passed. The attacker had already exfiltrated sensitive data and was attempting to escalate privileges.

Had AI-driven threat detection been in place, the attack wouldn't have progressed this far.

AI would have immediately detected that the developer had never accessed the repository from that location before. It would have correlated the sudden spike in data transfer with the attempted MFA bypass. Instead of waiting for an analyst to piece the logs together, the system would have recognized the pattern instantly.

A risk score would have been assigned within seconds. Automated response actions could have been triggered—

freezing the account, blocking further access, and alerting the SOC with a fully mapped-out timeline of the incident.

This is how AI transforms threat detection. It doesn't just flag isolated events. It connects activity across different systems, identifying patterns in real time. It reduces dwell time, eliminates manual log correlation, and allows SOC analysts to stop threats before they escalate.

In this chapter, we explore how AI-driven security detects and responds to threats faster than any human team can. From context-aware threat scoring to autonomous containment, AI is reshaping the way modern SOCs defend against cyberattacks.

The modern SOC faces an uphill battle. Cyberattacks are faster, more automated, and more coordinated than ever. Yet, many SOCs are still stuck responding with manual processes; analysts jumping between dozens of dashboards, correlating logs manually, and following cumbersome playbooks. This gap between attack speed and response speed is where AI becomes a game-changer.

With Kindo and WhiteRabbitNeo, incident response shifts from a slow, human-dependent process to a seamless collaboration between human analysts and AI-driven automation — where answers are just a search away in human language. The AI takes on the initial heavy lifting, parsing massive amounts of logs, correlating alerts across multiple tools, and even initiating containment actions in the critical first minutes after an attack is detected.

Kindo can automatically isolate compromised systems, block malicious IP addresses, revoke compromised credentials, and trigger forensic data collection — all in minutes. This reduces the time to containment (TTC) by up to 75%, turning what once took an hour into an action that happens almost instantly.

This also reduces one of the biggest hidden costs of incident response, reinventing security policies and workflows every time an incident occurs. In many SOCs, lessons learned from incidents are documented but rarely translated into immediate updates for detection and response logic. With Kindo, this process is automated. Instead of relying on manual intervention, Kindo's agents apply updates in real time, ensuring that policies and playbooks remain effective and up to date. Any deviation from security policies is immediately identified and addressed, allowing the SOC to adapt dynamically without requiring analysts to rewrite rules manually.

From Triage to Root Cause in Record Time

Traditional SOCs often get bogged down trying to reconstruct exactly what happened during an incident. Analysts have to hop between endpoint tools, network logs, email security alerts, and cloud telemetry—manually piecing together the story.

AI, and specifically Kindo, changes this narrative. Kindo's automated root cause analysis (RCA) capability automatically stitches together all relevant data into a timeline of the full attack chain, showing exactly how the intrusion started, where it spread, and what assets were impacted. Analysts no longer need to guess or manually search; the AI does it for them.

This automation gives analysts clarity faster, enabling them to move directly into remediation and lessons learned—rather than wasting hours in log diving.

This shift to AI-driven incident response isn't just about speed—it's about consistency and precision. In traditional

SOC processes, every analyst might approach incident triage slightly differently, leading to inconsistent outcomes, especially during high-pressure incidents like ransomware outbreaks. With AI-powered solutions like Kindo, every incident starts with the same level of enriched intelligence, and every initial response follows proven, adaptive workflows, ensuring that the quality of the response is no longer dependent on who happens to be on shift.

One of the biggest hidden costs of incident response is reinventing the wheel every time an attack occurs. In many SOCs, analysts document lessons learned in after-action reports, but those insights rarely make their way back into detection logic or response processes.

With Kindo, this feedback loop is streamlined. Each incident contributes to refining detection models, correlation logic, and response playbooks, ensuring that security processes improve over time. This allows SOC teams to focus on strategic decision-making rather than constantly rewriting detection rules.

From Incident Response to the Future of Continuous Learning

One of the hidden benefits of AI-accelerated incident response is how each incident enriches future detections. Traditional SOCs struggle to learn from past incidents because documentation is often incomplete, and lessons learned rarely make their way back into detection rules.

Kindo addresses this by automatically capturing incident context, response actions, and root cause findings into its knowledge base. Each incident is logged and can be used to enhance the system's understanding of attacker techniques, improving future detections and response strategies. This streamlined feedback loop strengthens SOC resilience, ensuring that security teams don't have to manually update detection logic after every new attack.

This process is especially valuable in an evolving threat landscape, where attackers constantly refine their methods. With Kindo, detection and response mechanisms dynamically adapt to emerging threats—aligning with real-world attack trends at scale.

The true power of continuous learning in SOCs will emerge in the future, when AI systems can autonomously refine themselves at machine speed. While traditional SOC processes relied on fragmented updates — one analyst adjusting a rule, another adding an entry to an internal threat library — Kindo's audit trail of AI actions and human use systematically integrates insights from every incident across tools and teams.

This continuous feedback loop combined with real time internet access to up-to-date information is essential in countering AI-enhanced threats, where adversaries evolve just as quickly. As attackers experiment with AI-generated polymorphic malware and deepfake-based social engineering, Kindo controlled AI's can refine its detection models in parallel, improving its ability to identify early-stage anomalies and predict future attack patterns. This shifts the SOC from a reactive function to an intelligence-driven, self-improving security operation — one that doesn't just respond faster but understands threats more deeply with every attack.

Case Study — From Hours to Minutes at a Critical Infrastructure SOC

A real-world example from Kindo's deployments highlights this transformation. A large critical infrastructure provider faced a ransomware attack that targeted their remote engineering workstations. Before Kindo, their average time to detect and contain (MTTD/MTTC) was over 4 hours, largely due to manual triage and coordination across siloed tools.

After integrating Kindo, the SOC reduced that response time to under 30 minutes, cutting containment time by over 80%. The AI not only detected the lateral movement faster but also initiated containment across both on-prem endpoints and cloud VMs, all without waiting for human approval.

This efficiency gain didn't just protect systems — it freed up analysts to focus on threat hunting and process improvement, raising the overall maturity of the SOC.

Beyond Response — Automating Post-Incident Cleanup

Incident response doesn't end with containment. Systems need to be fully cleaned, logs preserved for forensics, and findings documented for future learning. Traditionally, this cleanup process is labor-intensive, with analysts manually restoring systems, documenting artifacts, and updating detection rules.

Kindo streamlines post-incident operations by generating forensic reports, refining detection algorithms, and recommending policy adjustments to prevent future incidents. This is AI-augmented resilience in action. Analyzing each event to strengthen defenses for the next, ensuring the SOC evolves with every challenge faced.

What's often overlooked in the post-incident phase is the sheer administrative overhead it creates for SOC teams. After containment, analysts are expected to manually document every action taken, write comprehensive reports for leadership, update threat intelligence feeds, and in some cases, even manually tune detection rules based on what was learned. This post-incident effort is rarely standardized and almost always prone to gaps, inconsistencies, or missed follow-ups. This is where an AI-powered automation platform like Kindo can help, by automating much of this cleanup; it generates forensic-grade incident reports, complete with a visual timeline, mapped tactics, and response actions taken, ensuring documentation is accurate, complete, and immediately useful for future learning.

Additionally, Kindo doesn't just close the case and move on; it automatically extracts the key lessons from every incident and feeds them directly back into its detection and response information sources. If a new attacker TTP (Tactic, Technique, or Procedure) was observed during the incident, that behavior becomes part of Kindo's detection DNA, meaning future variations of the same attack can be identified faster and earlier. This kind of self-reinforcing learning loop is what allows modern SOCs to get smarter, not just faster, every single day.

Kindo is designed to be flexible and scalable, enabling organizations to avoid vendor lock-in while achieving rapid time-to-value. Its multi-modal, multi-model architecture supports both self-managed deployments and SaaS delivery, seamlessly integrating with existing enterprise infrastructure. By leveraging its AI-powered automation and orchestration capabilities, Kindo enhances security operations across multiple domains.

Kindo's Use Cases and Applications

- **Incident Response:** Kindo accelerates detection, triage, and remediation by automating threat correlation across sources and response workflows, reducing mean time to detect (MTTD) and mean time to respond (MTTR).

- **Infrastructure as Code (IaC) Security:** Automates security checks in cloud and DevOps environments, identifies misconfigurations and policy violations in Terraform, Kubernetes, and CI/CD pipelines.

- **IT Security/Ops:** Enhances operational security by integrating with SIEM, EDR, and firewall solutions, providing real-time security intelligence and automated response to mitigate threats.

- **Root Cause Analysis (RCA) / Identity & Access Management (IAM):** Kindo helps security teams trace incidents back to their origin, correlating identity-related events to detect privilege escalations and unauthorized access.

- **Vulnerability Management:** Prioritizes vulnerabilities based on real-world threat intelligence, automates workflow patches and integrates with VM solutions to drive ongoing risk reduction.

- **Cloud Security Posture Management (CSPM) / Cloud-Native Application Protection Platform (CNAPP):** Enables real-time visibility into cloud security risks, enforcing compliance and identifying misconfigurations in multi-cloud environments.
- **Penetration Testing:** Supports red teams by automating reconnaissance, threat simulation, and post-exploitation analysis, allowing for faster security assessments and continuous validation of defenses.

This structured approach ensures Kindo is not just another AI tool but an integral component of modern security operations, helping organizations stay ahead of evolving threats while reducing operational complexity.

Human Oversight Where It Matters

Despite all these automation capabilities, Kindo is not replacing human analysts. Rather, it's amplifying their strengths. Instead of wasting time on routine containment or root cause tasks, analysts focus on the why, interpreting attacker intent, understanding motives, and identifying underlying vulnerabilities in business processes.

This human-machine partnership, where AI handles grunt work and analysts focus on high-level decision-making is the future of incident response. It reduces burnout, improves morale, and raises the overall strategic value of the SOC.

Even with the most advanced AI handling detection, correlation, and response automation, human oversight remains critical. But the role of humans shifts dramatically in an AI-first SOC. Instead of analysts acting as manual processors, they become strategic interpreters, focusing on understanding attacker intent, validating high-confidence incidents, and deciding how to adapt defenses for evolving threats. With Kindo handling the time-consuming data assembly and initial triage, human expertise is applied exactly where it matters most, interpreting context, judging potential business impact, and shaping long-term defensive strategy.

This human-AI collaboration also becomes a critical safeguard in ensuring that automation itself does not drift off-course. Every time analysts override or enrich Kindo's recommendations, that feedback logs directly into Kindo's audit trail, providing a powerful data source for refining future decisions. This creates a human-guided learning cycle, where AI learns faster thanks to human input, and humans

118

benefit from AI's speed and scale. The result is a symbiotic SOC, where humans and machines don't compete, they complement and enhance each other, combining machine-speed processing with human intuition and business understanding.

In a world where adversaries are constantly innovating, using everything from AI-generated phishing campaigns to automated exploit kits, the old ways of incident response simply can't keep up. AI-powered platforms like Kindo are no longer optional; they are essential.

By combining real-time automation and seamless integration with existing tools, Kindo ensures that your SOC isn't just reacting, it's responding faster than the attackers can pivot. And in today's world, that's the difference between containment and catastrophe.

Chapter Six

How to Thrive with AI and Autonomous Agents

Lina had been working in the SOC for almost six years. She had seen it all; ransomware outbreaks, insider threats, sophisticated phishing campaigns, but nothing compared to what happened that Monday morning.

The team was still recovering from the weekend shift when a critical alert hit their SIEM dashboard: Unusual data transfer detected. At first glance, it seemed routine, just another system backup. But something felt off.

The logs showed large volumes of data leaving a sensitive internal server, but the process name was one Lina didn't recognize. Checking the source machine, she realized something alarming, it belonged to a CFO's assistant, someone who had no reason to be moving large files.

As she started digging through logs, another alert popped up: Privileged account access granted to an unmanaged endpoint. A sinking feeling crept in. Was this an insider threat? A compromised account?

The problem wasn't figuring out that something was wrong, the problem was time. SOC tools could detect anomalies, but they couldn't connect the dots fast enough. Lina had to manually correlate logs across different platforms: SIEM, EDR, NDR, identity management, while the attack was still unfolding in real-time.

By the time she had enough evidence to escalate, the exfiltration was complete.

That was the last breach before the organization finally adopted AI-powered autonomous SOC capabilities. The difference was night and day.

Had Lina been using AI-driven threat detection, the system would have:

- *Instantly recognized* that the assistant's credentials were being used in an unusual pattern.

- *Correlated* the privilege escalation with a suspicious remote access attempt.
- *Blocked the data transfer automatically,* stopping the breach before it even began.

Instead of racing to keep up, Lina would have had the incident flagged, investigated, and contained within minutes, before any real damage occurred.

This is the new reality of AI-driven SOCs. AI doesn't replace analysts like Lina, it empowers them. It filters out noise, connects seemingly unrelated events, and automates response actions, allowing security teams to focus on strategy rather than chaos.

In this chapter, we'll explore how SOCs can thrive in an era of AI and autonomous agents, leveraging intelligent automation, real-time decision-making, and human-AI collaboration to stay ahead of evolving threats.

There was a time when incident response felt like trying to catch rainwater with a sieve; alerts pouring in from every direction, analysts drowning in noise, and playbooks that looked great on paper but crumbled when reality hit. Incident response was reactive, slow, and often chaotic. And let's be honest, most of us were just hoping the storm would pass before things got too messy.

Fast forward to today, and it's a completely different story. AI and autonomous agents are the lifeline modern SOCs lean on. They don't just make things faster; they make incident response smarter, calmer, and in many cases, self-driving. That's the real game changer: it's not just automation anymore, its autonomous decision-making backed by learning systems that evolve with every single incident.

This is exactly where an AI-first security platform like Kindo can help, as a trusted partner in the fight. With Kindo's AI-driven SecOps capabilities, incident detection is fully automated, yes; but that's just the warm-up act. The real magic happens when Kindo's autonomous agents start weaving together stories from raw data: endpoint signals, cloud logs, network telemetry, even user behavior. And they don't just detect incidents; they interpret what's happening, what's likely coming next, and what action makes the most sense, all in real time.

No more waiting for analysts to connect the dots at 3 AM. Kindo triggers response playbooks automatically tailored not just to the type of threat, but to the actual context: which systems are affected, who the users are, and what's considered normal for this environment.

And these playbooks? They're not static documents gathering dust. Kindo dynamically refines them based on current threat intelligence, past incidents, and real-time situational awareness. It's like having an analyst who doesn't sleep, doesn't miss anything, and optimizes its responses with every attack.

But Kindo's impact extends beyond incident response. Its AI agents are transforming threat hunting, compliance, and proactive security operations. By scanning for vulnerabilities, enforcing Governance, Risk, and Compliance (GRC) standards, and enhancing security automation, Kindo helps organizations maintain a robust security posture.

AI-driven capabilities also optimize DevOps security, analyzing and remediating vulnerabilities in Infrastructure as Code (IaC) templates, identifying misconfigurations, and suggesting fixes—ensuring that security is embedded into every stage of development.

Integrating an uncensored security and infrastructure trained AI model like WhiteRabbitNeo into this ecosystem adds another layer of intelligence. As an uncensored, open-source AI model designed for offensive and defensive cybersecurity, WhiteRabbitNeo assists in tasks like penetration testing, vulnerability detection, and remediation. It understands threat intelligence, software engineering, and infrastructure as code, enabling it to craft novel attacks in dozens of programming and scripting languages and provide immediate remediation for detected threats. WhiteRabbitNeo is also an excellent language translator which helps analysts deal with the global threat space more effectively.

With WhiteRabbitNeo, security practitioners can automate some of the most challenging and time-consuming tasks they face. For instance, it can help blue team professionals research threat intelligence, construct search queries and scripts for popular SIEM systems, and even remediate threats with automated IDS and IPS rules.

Of course, the goal isn't just to speed up responses—that's table stakes. Thriving with AI and autonomous agents means building a SOC that gets smarter every single day. With every resolved incident, the system doesn't just close a ticket—it stores data for future learning adjust and strengthens its defenses. This is how resilience is built: faster today, smarter tomorrow.

And this is why Kindo isn't just a solution you deploy, it's the solution that grows with you, becoming part of your team. It doesn't replace your analysts; it gives them breathing room to focus on what really matters: thinking ahead, hunting for threats, and designing better defenses.

By leveraging AI and autonomous agents, deploying AI-first solutions like Kindo and WhiteRabbitNeo transform the SOC into a dynamic intelligence system that refines its detection, adapts to evolving threats, and enhances response strategies with every incident. This holistic approach ensures that organizations are not just reacting to threats but proactively strengthening their defenses, setting a new standard for what a modern SOC can achieve.

Understanding Agentic Security and AI Agents

As artificial intelligence advances, one of the most transformative concepts in cybersecurity is Agentic Security: an approach that leverages AI agents to autonomously detect, analyze, and respond to threats in real time. Unlike traditional security automation, which follows predefined rules and workflows, agentic AI operates with greater autonomy, adjusting its responses based on real-time insights and evolving threats. While it enhances adaptability, its decision-making processes are refined through structured data, analyst feedback, and global threat intelligence, ensuring security teams maintain oversight while benefiting from AI-driven efficiency.

What Are AI Agents?

AI agents are autonomous systems designed to perform specific tasks with minimal human intervention. Unlike conventional AI models that require direct input and predefined parameters to function, AI agents operate with a level of self-governance. They interpret high-level objectives, analyze real-time data, and make decisions based on contextual understanding. These agents can be deployed singly or as part of a multi-agent system, where multiple specialized AI agents collaborate to enhance cybersecurity operations.

AI agents play a crucial role in automating tasks such as threat detection, risk assessment, and incident response. They can process massive amounts of security telemetry, correlate disparate data points, and execute predefined or adaptive mitigation strategies without waiting for human validation. This shift from static deterministic automation to dynamic, intelligent, self-driven security operations is what defines the rise of agentic security.

How Agentic Security Enhances Cyber Defense

Agentic security leverages AI agents to create an adaptive, proactive security model. Instead of relying on static rules and human oversight to analyze threats, agentic AI can autonomously detect anomalies, investigate suspicious behavior, and take real-time action to neutralize risks. This reduces response times significantly, minimizing the window of opportunity for attackers.

For example, an AI agent within a SOC can monitor endpoint activity in real time, detect unusual patterns indicative of an attack, and autonomously quarantine affected assets. Simultaneously, another AI agent can initiate a forensic investigation, gathering intelligence on attack techniques and refining detection rules to prevent similar incidents in the future. This approach shifts cybersecurity from a reactive model, where analysts manually analyze and respond, to a proactive and autonomous framework. By doing so, agentic security helps organizations stay ahead of advanced threats, reduces analyst burnout, and enhances overall security resilience.

Kindo and WhiteRabbitNeo: Revolutionizing Agentic Security

Kindo is at the forefront of this transformation, deploying an army of AI agents to enable a quicker, more reliable approach to security. By leveraging Kindo's multi-agent system, a single security operator can build, manage, and execute powerful SecOps workflows at 10X the speed of larger teams running traditional SOARs and DevOps tooling. WhiteRabbitNeo, as the first open-source, uncensored AI model built for DevSecOps teams, further enhances this ecosystem by providing deep automation, intelligent response mechanisms, and adaptive threat analysis. Together, these innovations empower SOCs to operate at machine speed, ensuring faster, smarter, and more efficient security operations without increasing operational complexity.

With the rapid rise of AI-driven cyber threats, agentic security is no longer a futuristic vision, it is becoming a necessity in modern SOC environments, ensuring that organizations can operate at machine speed while maintaining full situational awareness and control.

The Expanding AI Infrastructure: A Market Shift Driving Agentic Security

The adoption of AI-driven security isn't happening in isolation. The broader AI infrastructure market is growing at an exponential rate, driven by enterprise demand for smarter, faster, and more scalable solutions. According to MarketsandMarkets, the AI infrastructure market is set to expand significantly, fueled by the need for autonomous decision-making systems that reduce dependency on manual processes.

The rapid evolution of AI-powered security is driven by the same needs. Security teams are drowning in complexity. Every tool they use, SIEM, EDR, SOAR, vulnerability management, IAM, generates massive volumes of alerts and telemetry. Manually sifting through this data is no longer viable. Enterprises need AI-driven solutions that do more than automate tasks, they need AI that orchestrates security at scale, eliminating inefficiencies.

This shift has fueled demand for AI as a Service (AIaaS) and Agents as a Service (AaaS), where security platforms no longer operate as static rule-based systems but as evolving, self-improving AI-driven ecosystems. Instead of hiring larger SOC teams to manage an ever-expanding security stack, organizations are now leveraging autonomous AI agents to take over the most time-consuming security operations—threat detection, response, root cause analysis, and incident triage.

Kindo's Role in the AI-Powered SOC

Kindo was built in response to this exact problem. Unlike traditional SOARs or SIEMs that require constant fine-tuning, Kindo leverages agentic AI models including WhiteRabbitNeo, to automate adaptable SecOps workflows with precision.

✔ **Real-time adaptive response:** AI agents automatically detect, correlate, and respond to threats—minimizing the need for manual triage.

✔ **Multi-modal AI infrastructure:** Kindo integrates multiple AI models, ensuring organizations can tailor security workflows without vendor lock-in.

✔ **Enterprise-ready at scale:** Unlike legacy security tools that struggle with large-scale cloud adoption, Kindo orchestrates security seamlessly across hybrid and multi-cloud environments.

The AI infrastructure boom isn't just a trend—it's a fundamental transformation in how security teams operate. With AI now driving real-time, adaptive security operations, enterprises must move beyond traditional, static security models and embrace an agentic, AI-first approach.

Automate Incident Detection with Context Built-In

Traditionally, incident detection meant log aggregation, signature matching, and a flood of alerts that forced analysts into constant firefighting. But with Kindo, the game changes. Alerts don't just pop up, they arrive pre-analyzed, enriched with context from across your environment: endpoint, network, cloud, even identity systems. Instead of asking, *"What just happened?"* your analysts get a clear, actionable answer—what happened, why it matters, and what to do next: in a way that's easy to understand and act on.

In Kindo, the moment an anomaly surfaces, whether it's a suspicious login at an odd hour or a lateral movement pattern across servers, the correct response workflow is triggered, pre-filling incident tickets, linking relevant logs, and recommending next steps. This isn't just basic automation: it's contextual orchestration. It's like having an ultra-efficient digital SOC analyst who works at machine speed.

Faster Root Cause Analysis and Response

One of the biggest drains on SOC productivity is time wasted digging for root causes. The right AI tool is the difference between investigating with a flashlight and seeing the entire attack story in daylight. Traditionally, an analyst might pivot between five or more tools—log management, threat intelligence, EDR consoles, network monitoring, and more—just to reconstruct what happened. With Kindo, that grunt work is gone.

AI-based playbooks automatically correlate artifacts, map out attack paths, and surface the root cause without requiring manual deep dives. The autonomous agents don't just see a suspicious process—they trace back to who triggered it, what was touched, and what it connects to next.

Cutting MTTR in Half (and then Some)

It's one thing to detect faster; it's another to respond smartly. Traditional SOCs measure Mean Time to Respond in hours, even days, because they rely heavily on manual handoffs and coordination across teams. Kindo rewrites that script.

By integrating directly with ticketing systems like ServiceNow, Zendesk or Jira, and leveraging SOAR capabilities, Kindo doesn't just detect and diagnose—it acts. Isolation, containment, and even proactive countermeasures can kick off autonomously. And because Kindo logs every action directly into the incident record, your compliance reports practically write themselves.

AI Fast-Tracking Incident Response—The Real-World Story

To truly understand how AI and autonomous agents transform incident response, it helps to step into the shoes of someone who's already lived through the change. That's where Peter from Aireon comes in.

A couple of years back, Peter Clay (CISO Aireon)'s SOC life looked like what most of us have lived through, constant alerts, too many false positives, and the soul-crushing grind of manually connecting dots between disconnected tools. Every incident was a puzzle dumped on his desk, with half the pieces missing.

When Aireon introduced Kindo into their SOC, Peter wasn't expecting magic, but what he got was close. Incidents didn't just show up as alerts anymore. They came pre-wrapped with context: who triggered the event, what system was affected, what behavior patterns matched, and what historical incidents resembled this.

The biggest shift was how much of the manual triage disappeared overnight. Kindo's autonomous agents didn't just feed data into a dashboard—they actually made recommendations right alongside the alerts. Peter wasn't guessing anymore; he was confirming. And with every confirmed incident, Kindo's playbooks updated themselves, learning from each response to become sharper next time.

Within months, Aireon's Mean Time to Respond (MTTR) dropped by more than half—not because analysts worked faster, but because Kindo cleared their plate. Peter's team wasn't scrambling anymore — they were planning, hunting, and improving the whole process.

But the real win wasn't just in the speed, it was in confidence. Every decision Peter's team made came with a clear audit trail from Kindo: why the AI flagged something, which artifacts were involved, and what past cases shaped its recommendation. No black boxes, no hidden logic — just trustworthy automation that earned its place in the team.

Peter said, "We used Kindo to accelerate and simplify our threat hunting processes, which enabled us to increase the value of our existing SIEM infrastructure and identify issues before they became real problems. The time and potential impact have resulted in a cost savings of over $2M per year and growing."

Trust and Accountability — Keeping AI Transparent

In modern SOCs, AI-driven automation must be reliable, explainable, and accountable. Security teams need full visibility into how decisions are made — whether it's detecting threats, enforcing access controls, optimizing workflows, or automating compliance checks.

With Kindo and WhiteRabbitNeo, every action is fully traceable. Analysts can see why an alert was prioritized, what data influenced a decision, and how automated responses were triggered. Whether it's isolating a compromised endpoint, refining threat intelligence, or recommending security policies, every step is logged, auditable, and explainable.

This level of transparency ensures AI doesn't operate in a black box but as a trusted partner. Organizations maintain control while benefiting from autonomous speed, knowing that every action is accountable and based on real-time risk assessment. In cybersecurity, trust isn't just about compliance—it's about confidence in every decision, every mitigation, and every layer of defense. With AI-first solutions like Kindo and WhiteRabbitNeo, SOCs become not just faster, but smarter and more transparent.

The True Value—It's Not Just Faster, It's Smarter

If there's one thing Peter would tell any SOC team considering AI, it's this: the real power isn't in the automation, it's in how that automation frees you to be proactive.

Before Kindo, Peter's team spent their days reacting. After Kindo, they had the time and space to think ahead, to refine detection rules, run tabletop exercises, and sharpen playbooks. They stopped chasing alerts and started designing resilience.

That's the shift every SOC need, from firefighting to foresight. And that's how you don't just survive the next incident, you thrive through it.

From Faster Response to Business Resilience

In today's digital-first economy, cyber resilience is business resilience. Downtime, reputational damage, and financial loss are the real concerns keeping executives up at night—not Mean Time to Respond metrics.

Tools like Kindo and WhiteRabbitNeo transform SOCs from reactive security hubs into strategic business enablers. By leveraging AI-driven automation and iterative optimization based on historical data and real-time insights, they don't just accelerate incident response: they help reduce the frequency and impact of security disruptions altogether.

This translates directly into operational continuity, regulatory compliance, and risk reduction. With faster containment, fewer repeat incidents, and AI-driven predictive insights, businesses can protect revenue streams, maintain customer trust, and ensure uninterrupted service delivery.

Kindo doesn't just make security teams more efficient, it turns cybersecurity into a business advantage, aligning SecOps with corporate objectives and ensuring resilience at every level of the organization.

Keeping Humans in the Loop — Because Judgment Still Matters

AI enhances security operations, but human expertise remains irreplaceable. Analysts bring context, strategic thinking, and business awareness, factors AI alone cannot fully grasp.

Kindo frees analysts from alert fatigue by curating incidents, providing full context, and recommending actions, so security teams focus on high-impact decisions rather than sifting through noise. Automated workflows accelerate detection and response, but the final call always belongs to the human expert.

This synergy—AI for efficiency and humans for judgment—creates a resilient, high-performing SOC where analysts work smarter, not harder. Instead of being overwhelmed, they stay ahead, ensuring security decisions align with business priorities. Rather than automation vs. expertise, it's the power of both, working together.

Building Trust—From Automation to Partnership

The technology is important, but it's trust that makes AI stick in a SOC. Trust grows when the team sees automation 'working for them', not 'instead of them'. The more they interact with it, validate its decisions, and even challenge it, the more that sense of partnership builds.

Over time, automation stops being something to fear—and starts being the trusted teammate who never sleeps, never misses a log, and learns from every case. That's the shift every modern SOC need, from 'resistance to reliance'. And it's not about replacing analysts, it's about freeing them to focus on what humans do best

- seeing the big picture,
- asking the hard questions, and
- staying ahead of the next attack.

From Surviving Alerts to Thriving with Intelligence

A modern SOC must go beyond just reacting — it needs to:

- anticipate,
- adapt, and
- strengthen

with every incident. Security operations should evolve dynamically, refining detection logic and optimizing response strategies based on real-time threats and emerging attack patterns. By integrating intelligence-driven automation, SOCs can stay ahead of adversaries rather than merely keeping up.

Kindo and WhiteRabbitNeo transform SOCs into intelligence-driven ecosystems. Every incident feed into a learning loop, enhancing detection accuracy and automating responses with greater precision. Analysts start with a complete, context-rich incident view, eliminating hours of manual correlation and enabling faster, more strategic decision-making.

With AI-driven workflows, the SOC moves from constant firefighting to a proactive security model, ensuring resilience, minimizing disruptions, and keeping businesses ahead of emerging threats.

Resilience Beyond the SOC—Why Faster Response Strengthens the Whole Business

Every incident isn't just a security event—it's a business event. A disrupted application, a compromised account, or an exposed dataset can trigger

- financial losses,
- reputational harm, and
- operational slowdowns.

This is why an AI-driven SOC doesn't just secure infrastructure—it strengthens business resilience.

With Kindo and WhiteRabbitNeo, security operations become faster, more intelligent, and seamlessly aligned with business priorities. Automated threat detection, real-time risk assessment, and proactive mitigation help teams across the organization stay ahead of disruptions. IT restores services faster, compliance teams maintain audit-ready records, and leadership gains real-time visibility into security posture. Beyond speed, organizations need accountability and assurance. Every decision, from access control enforcement to threat containment, is logged, explainable, and repeatable—providing transparency for regulatory audits, executive briefings, and strategic refinement. With this level of visibility, cybersecurity becomes a business enabler rather than just a cost center, reducing risks, ensuring uptime, and protecting revenue while strengthening overall resilience.

This is the true impact of AI-driven SecOps—not just faster response, but a stronger, more resilient business that is ready for the future.

Thriving Means Evolving—And It Never Stops

The truth is there's no final destination for security. New technologies emerge, attackers adapt, business priorities shift. But when your incident response is built on AI-driven learning, your SOC can evolve just as fast. Every incident makes the system smarter, every response refines the process, and every lesson learned strengthens the next decision.

That's what thriving with AI and autonomous agents truly means. It's not a one-time upgrade, but an evolving collaboration between human expertise and machine intelligence. It creates a SOC that refines its strategies, adapts to emerging threats, and remains ready not just to respond, but to lead the way forward.

With this, Chapter 6 comes to a close; but the journey to smarter, faster, and more resilient security operations is just getting started. In the next chapter, we'll look at how this technology-driven transformation fits into the broader ethics conversation; ensuring that even as machines take on more responsibility, transparency, fairness, and accountability remain at the heart of everything we do.

Chapter Seven

Future Trends: AI-Enabled Security is an Ever-Evolving Landscape

The following is a fictionalized scenario, illustrating the potential future of AI-driven cybersecurity based on emerging trends and technological advancements.

The 2027 Global Cybersecurity Summit in Washington, D.C., was meant to be a showcase of the latest advancements in AI-driven security. Cybersecurity leaders, regulators, and executives from multinational corporations gathered to discuss emerging threats, regulatory challenges, and the evolving role of artificial intelligence in security operations.

On the main stage, an industry-leading AI security vendor demonstrated its next-generation autonomous SOC, showcasing how AI-driven behavioral analytics and machine learning models could predict and neutralize cyber threats in real time. The audience watched as a simulated ransomware attack unfolded, designed to demonstrate how AI could detect, isolate, and mitigate advanced threats.

Then, something unexpected happened.

As the AI system processed the simulated attack, it abruptly flagged an active, real-world breach attempt—one that was not part of the demonstration. A sophisticated, adaptive adversary had been watching the live event remotely, waiting for the perfect moment to strike. The attack targeted the demonstration system itself, attempting to manipulate its AI models in real-time.

For a brief, tense moment, uncertainty filled the room. Was this an elaborate coincidence? Or had the event's high-profile nature attracted a deliberate, real-world cyberattack?

Then, the AI-driven security system responded—without waiting for human intervention.

- It isolated the compromised node within milliseconds, cutting off the attacker's access before any data exfiltration could begin.

- It executed dynamic threat modeling, rapidly analyzing the attack pattern and predicting the adversary's next likely move.
- It adapted security controls on the fly, deploying countermeasures that were not pre-scripted in any playbook but instead generated in real-time based on the evolving attack.

By the time human analysts reviewed the incident, the AI had already:

- Neutralized the breach attempt.
- Investigated the attack vector.
- Documented the entire sequence of events for forensic analysis.

The event became an inflection point in cybersecurity — a defining moment when AI was no longer just an assistant but an autonomous force multiplier.

AI is No Longer Just a Tool — It's a Force Multiplier

Traditional security models relied on human analysts making decisions, with AI assisting through automation. That dynamic is now shifting.

Modern AI models no longer just detect threats faster — they predict them, simulate their impact, and preemptively strengthen defenses before an attack even occurs.

This evolution is redefining security architectures:

- AI isn't just monitoring for threats; it's proactively conducting attack simulations to identify vulnerabilities before adversaries can exploit them.
- AI isn't just analyzing logs; its learning from real-world breaches and adjusting its defense strategies autonomously.
- AI isn't just assisting analysts; it's making first-level security decisions, reducing time-to-containment from hours to minutes or, in some cases, from minutes to milliseconds — as demonstrated in real-world AI-driven security research by Google DeepMind and MIT's CSAIL (Cybersecurity and AI Laboratory).

These AI-driven SOCs are not futuristic, they are emerging now. Companies like Kindo, Darktrace, CrowdStrike, and Microsoft are already pioneering autonomous threat detection and response, reducing containment times from an industry average of four hours to under five minutes in real-world incidents.

The question is no longer whether AI can improve security. The question is how fast organizations can trust AI to take control in moments of crisis.

Infrastructure Security is Becoming AI-Driven

This transformation isn't limited to SOC operations. It extends deep into infrastructure security, DevOps, and cloud governance.

- AI is hardening Infrastructure as Code (IaC) in real time, scanning configurations, detecting vulnerabilities, and suggesting remediations before deployment.
- AI is orchestrating zero-trust policies dynamically, adjusting access controls based on real-time risk analysis.
- AI is transforming security from reactive to proactive by analyzing threat intelligence feeds, global attack patterns, and industry-specific vulnerabilities to refine detection and response strategies.

AI first Kindo and WhiteRabbitNeo: Pioneering the Next Generation of AI Security and Infrastructure Control

Kindo isn't just responding to cyber threats—it's actively reshaping security strategies by embedding autonomous AI into every layer of cybersecurity.

With WhiteRabbitNeo, security teams aren't just detecting threats; they're anticipating them, modeling attack paths, and deploying adaptive countermeasures—all in real time.

The future of AI in security isn't just about automation. It's about orchestration, prediction, and real-time adaptation. It's about building security frameworks that can think, react, and evolve faster than attackers can.

And in this new era of AI-enabled security, the organizations that stay ahead will be those that embrace intelligent adaptation, proactive defense, and AI-driven resilience to counter evolving threats effectively.

Because the next cyber war won't be fought with static rules and traditional defenses—it will be AI against AI, and only the most adaptive systems will survive.

The future of AI in cybersecurity is not just about automation. It's about creating a security function that analyzes threats in real time, refines its defenses based on evolving risks, and strengthens the organization's digital fabric without waiting for human intervention. That's the future we're walking into, and the smartest SOCs are already preparing for it.

In the future we're heading toward, infrastructure won't wait to be secured after deployment — it will be designed secure from the start, with AI monitoring, analyzing, and strengthening it in real time. This isn't just about adding security checks to DevOps pipelines; it's about embedding intelligent security into the entire infrastructure lifecycle, where AI acts as a silent advisor at every stage.

Right now, most security reviews happen after the fact. Code gets written, infrastructure gets deployed, and then someone runs a scan to spot misconfigurations and vulnerabilities. By then, the gap between design and detection is already too wide. In the AI-driven future, this sequence flips. Security checks become part of the design process itself, and AI tools constantly read, interpret, and assess your IaC the moment it's committed.

Kindo is already laying the groundwork for this, helping security and DevOps teams connect detection and response into a seamless feedback loop. In the future, this will expand further—incident learnings will directly inform infrastructure hardening. For example, if a particular IAM misconfiguration led to a breach, Kindo's leveraging WhiteRabbitNeo AI will not only recommend the immediate fix but update future templates to automatically close that gap. Security will evolve from reacting to vulnerabilities to preventing them from ever existing.

This concept of continuous hardening isn't just a DevSecOps dream—it's becoming a practical reality. With every change made to your cloud environment, every line of IaC passes through an AI lens. Risk factors are highlighted, insecure patterns flagged, and secure-by-default alternatives might even be suggested. Instead of static compliance checklists, teams will have real-time, evolving security guidance— tailored to their environment, risk appetite, and actual incident history.

This is what true security by design looks like when AI is fully embedded into the lifecycle. It's not a separate process or a reactive scan—it's an integral part of how infrastructure is built, born secure and resilient against threats from the very first line of code.

The smartest organizations will no longer see security and infrastructure as separate disciplines. Instead, they will form one seamless flow, with AI acting as both architect and guardian—not just preventing attacks, but shaping environments where threats struggle to gain a foothold.

The Security Analyst of the Future—From Responder to Resilience Architect

The role of the security analyst is undergoing a profound transformation. In the past, security teams functioned as isolated units:

- reacting to alerts,
- responding to incidents, and
- conducting periodic compliance checks.

This reactive approach worked when threats evolved slowly, but in today's AI-driven, machine-speed threat landscape, traditional SOC workflows simply can't keep up.

The future of security isn't about chasing attackers: it's about staying ahead of them. Analysts of the future won't be logging divers or ticket closers. Instead, they will become

- architects of resilience,
- embedding security into every layer of infrastructure,
- processes, and
- business decisions.

AI-driven security, especially with platforms like Kindo, is breaking down operational silos, integrating security seamlessly into workflows, and creating an adaptive cycle that refines itself over time.

- Detection feeds directly into response.
- Response teaches prevention.
- Prevention shapes system design.

This end-to-end security loop ensures that AI-driven SOCs don't just react to threats but actively eliminate attack vectors before adversaries exploit them. Security analysts will transition from responders to risk designers, working alongside developers, cloud architects, and business leaders to create systems that are resilient by default.

Emerging Technologies and the Expanding Role of SOCs

As AI continues to reshape cybersecurity, SOCs must evolve to secure new and emerging technologies that are transforming the digital landscape. The threats of tomorrow will not only come from faster and more automated adversaries but also from the security gaps created by new technological breakthroughs.

While we have already discussed AI-driven threats in depth, there are other critical areas where SOCs must expand their expertise:

Web3.0 & Blockchain Security – The rise of decentralized applications (dApps) and smart contracts introduces new attack surfaces. SOCs must develop specialized blockchain security monitoring to detect vulnerabilities in decentralized finance (DeFi), tokenized assets, and smart contract logic flaws.

Quantum Computing & Cryptography – Quantum advancements threaten traditional encryption methods, making it essential for SOCs to adopt quantum-resistant cryptographic solutions. Preparing for post-quantum security isn't a choice, it's a necessity.

AI-Augmented Cyber Threats – We've already explored how adversaries are leveraging AI to automate and scale attacks, and we'll continue to discuss this throughout the book. The key takeaway is that SOCs must not just defend against AI-driven threats but actively use AI-powered solutions like Kindo to stay ahead — operating at machine speed, predicting attacks before they happen, and automating response workflows in real time.

Metaverse & Immersive AI Security – The Metaverse and AI-driven immersive environments bring new privacy and security challenges. SOCs will need to monitor avatar behavior, secure digital identities, and prevent AI-generated fraud in these new digital landscapes.

Fusion Technology & Industrial Cybersecurity – The emergence of nuclear fusion energy, bioinformatics, and advanced robotics requires SOCs to rethink industrial cybersecurity. Critical infrastructure protection will demand AI-driven anomaly detection, supply chain integrity monitoring, and predictive threat analysis to prevent cyber-physical attacks.

The future of AI in cybersecurity is not just about better detection and faster response—it will be shaped by how AI itself evolves. AI techniques are moving beyond simple pattern recognition and into adaptive learning models that can predict, defend, and automate security at an unprecedented scale.

Here's what's already shaping next-generation SOCs:

✔ **Reinforcement Learning (PPO, DQN, Q-Learning) –** These models are essential for attack path prediction and automated threat hunting. Imagine an AI that doesn't just react but actively simulates attacker behavior in real time, learning and adjusting its defensive strategies dynamically.

✔ **Generative Adversarial Networks (GANs) –** SOCs can simulate realistic attack scenarios using GANs, creating AI-powered red teams that run 24/7 to stress-test defenses before real attackers do.

✔ **Convolutional & Recurrent Neural Networks (CNNs & RNNs) –** These models excel at identifying hidden attack patterns in large-scale security datasets—from network traffic anomalies to insider threats—spotting subtle signals that human analysts might miss.

✔ **Natural Language Processing (NLP)** – SOCs deal with endless streams of threat reports, advisories, and intelligence feeds. NLP engines automate the extraction of actionable insights, turning unstructured data into structured intelligence that analysts can act on instantly.

✔ **Explainability & Trust Layers (SHAP & LIME)** – AI's biggest challenge is trust. Explainability tools like SHAP and LIME provide transparency, ensuring analysts understand why AI made a particular decision—a critical factor for AI adoption in cybersecurity.

The next evolution of SOCs isn't just about defending against today's threats: it's about securing a future where technology itself is constantly changing.

Kindo with WhiteRabbitNeo: Future-Proofing SOCs

As these new frontiers emerge, Kindo with WhiteRabbitNeo, ensures that SOCs remain adaptive, proactive, and resilient. By leveraging AI-driven automation, predictive analytics, and intelligent security orchestration, Kindo helps SOCs:

✔ **Anticipate and Mitigate Future Threats** – AI-powered predictive analytics foresee attack vectors before they occur, allowing preemptive defense.

✔ **Integrate Security into Emerging Technologies** – Quantum-resistant security, blockchain risk management, and AI-driven anomaly detection enable SOCs to secure the next wave of digital transformation.

✔ **Enhance Analyst Efficiency** – Automating low-level security operations allows analysts to focus on high-value security strategy, threat hunting, and risk modeling.

The future of cybersecurity isn't just about faster tools or smarter alerts, it's about a fundamental shift in mindset. The most advanced SOCs of tomorrow won't measure success by how quickly they respond to incidents, but by how few incidents they ever need to respond to.

With Kindo and WhiteRabbitNeo leading the way, security analysts are no longer just responders, they are becoming resilience architects, shaping a world where security is embedded, automated, and intelligent.

Predictions for the Future of SOCs

With all these technological advancements converging, the Security Operations Center of the future will look nothing like today's reactive command center. Based on the evolution patterns we've seen, here's where SOCs are heading:

- **More Engineering Workflows:** SOC teams will work side-by-side with DevOps and IT teams, influencing how systems are built from the ground up, ensuring security is embedded into the architecture itself.

- **Cross-Department Collaboration:** The invisible walls between security, IT, OT, and compliance will dissolve. Security will be everyone's job, with SOC playing a coordinating role rather than owning every step.

- **Machine Learning-Driven Detection:** Detection will evolve from static rules to dynamic models. Instead of manual tuning, SOCs will focus on curating training data, enabling AI to learn, adapt, and anticipate emerging attack techniques before they appear in the wild.

- **Collaborative Threat Intelligence Sharing:** SOCs won't just defend their own networks: they'll participate in community defense, sharing anonymized threat data across industries and geographies, so every attack caught by one SOC helps protect hundreds of others.

- **Outsourced Specialization:** Internal SOC teams will become leaner while external specialist services (like managed threat hunting or AI model tuning) will be brought in as needed. This hybrid approach balances cost, expertise, and agility.

- **AI-Driven Incident Triage:** Instead of humans sifting through alerts, AI will analyze and prioritize incidents automatically, ensuring that analysts only focus on the most critical cases.

- **Autonomous SOC Operations:** AI will take over first-line responses, automating containment, mitigation, and recovery—allowing SOCs to function more like autopilot systems that only escalate complex cases to human experts.

- **Cloud-Native Security Operations:** SOCs will be designed for cloud-first environments, leveraging scalable, cloud-native security solutions to monitor hybrid and multi-cloud infrastructures.

- **Zero Trust-Driven Monitoring:** SOCs will enforce Zero Trust principles, continuously verifying identities and access requests instead of relying on traditional perimeter-based security models.

- **AI-Augmented Decision Making:** AI will enhance human decision-making by providing deeper context, analyzing attacker behaviors, and suggesting the best response strategies in real time.

- **Threat Hunting as a Core Function:** Rather than just reacting to alerts, SOCs will proactively hunt for hidden threats using AI-driven anomaly detection and behavioral analytics.

- **Human-Free SOC Shift Operations:** SOC analysts won't have to stare at monitors 24/7 — AI will handle continuous monitoring, and humans will be engaged only when needed. Shift teams will still be on-call 24/7 but act as a backup rather than active watchers.

- **Adaptive Playbooks and Response Automation:** SOCs will move beyond static incident response plans to AI-driven adaptive playbooks that update automatically based on real-time attack patterns.

- **Defensive AI vs. Offensive AI Warfare:** Cybercriminals will weaponize AI to generate polymorphic malware, AI-powered phishing, and adaptive ransomware, requiring SOCs to counterattack with advanced AI defenses.

- **Supply Chain Risk Monitoring:** With the expanding digital ecosystem, SOCs will need to monitor third-party vendors, suppliers, and partners as part of their threat intelligence operations.

- **Adversarial AI Countermeasures:** Attackers will attempt to poison AI training datasets or manipulate machine learning models, making it essential for SOCs to develop AI integrity verification techniques.

- **Self-Healing Security Systems:** AI will drive automated security infrastructure that can detect vulnerabilities, patch itself, and reconfigure defenses without human intervention.

- **Global Threat Collaboration:** SOCs will operate beyond organizational boundaries, partnering with industry-wide AI security alliances to share real-time threat intelligence.

- **Cyber Resilience Over Prevention:** Instead of just blocking attacks, future SOCs will focus on ensuring business continuity by rapidly containing and recovering from security incidents.

- **Quantum-Resistant Security Strategies:** As quantum computing advances, SOCs will need to prepare for quantum-resistant cryptography and new approaches to securing encrypted data.

- **Virtual SOCs & Remote-First Operations:** The SOC workforce will shift toward remote and distributed teams, leveraging cloud-based collaboration tools and virtual security environments.

- **AI-Powered Forensics & Post-Breach Analysis:** Instead of manually reconstructing incidents, AI will automate digital forensics, rapidly analyzing attack timelines and providing actionable insights.

- **Behavior-Based Authentication & Monitoring:** Instead of relying on static credentials, SOCs will use continuous behavioral analysis to detect unauthorized access attempts in real time.

- **Ethical AI & Regulatory Compliance Automation:** With AI playing a bigger role in cybersecurity, SOCs will need built-in transparency, compliance tracking, and ethical AI frameworks to meet regulatory demands.

- **Predictive Defense Mechanisms:** Instead of just reacting to threats, AI will use predictive analytics to model potential attack scenarios and automatically harden security before an attack occurs.

- **Personalized AI Security Assistants:** SOC analysts will have AI-powered security copilots that assist in investigations, summarize incidents, and recommend mitigation steps tailored to each case.

Combined, it is the death of the traditional SOC as we know it.

In the future, SOCs will look more like an intelligent autopilot system, as seen with Kindo today, where AI handles most incidents end-to-end, only escalating the truly complex cases to humans. Security will become a background process: *always on, always learning, and largely invisible.*

Of course, technology alone isn't enough. The threat landscape isn't slowing down. Attackers will weaponize the same AI tools defenders rely on, leading to:

- Polymorphic malware that constantly evolves to bypass detection,
- AI-generated phishing campaigns that are highly personalized and context-aware, and

- Adaptive ransomware capable of changing its tactics in real time.

The Challenges SOCs Must Prepare For

To thrive in this AI-driven security landscape, SOCs need to address:

- **AI vs. AI Warfare:** Attackers are already leveraging AI to:
  - Probe defenses for weaknesses,
  - Craft highly convincing social engineering attacks, and
  - Bypass static security controls using real-time adaptation.
- **Supply Chain Blind Spots:** As ecosystem security becomes the new perimeter, SOCs must monitor not just their own environments but also third-party risks from partners, vendors, and service providers.
- **Adversarial AI:** Attackers will attempt to:
  - Poison training data to mislead AI models,
  - Disrupt detection algorithms, and
  - Exploit biases in machine learning pipelines to evade security tools.

- **Nation-State Grade Automation:** The scale and sophistication of nation-state cyber-attacks will filter down to cybercriminal groups, turning yesterday's advanced tactics into tomorrow's commodity threats.

- **Security Convergence:** The merging of physical and cyber security functions will require SOCs to adopt integrated strategies to address blended threats effectively.

- **Cloud Security Challenges:** As organizations migrate to cloud environments, SOCs must address:
  - Data residency regulations,
  - Unauthorized access to management interfaces, and
  - Encryption vulnerabilities in multi-cloud environments.

- **Operational Collaboration:** SOCs should engage in public-private partnerships to enhance cyber resilience, share real-time threat intelligence, and coordinate responses to cyber threats.

The AI Talent Dilemma – A Growing Risk

While AI is transforming cybersecurity, it also poses a significant risk to the cybersecurity talent pipeline.

Cybersecurity has become increasingly less beginner-friendly, making it difficult for junior professionals to enter the field. AI-driven automation is already replacing many entry-level tasks, which traditionally served as steppingstones for early-career security analysts. Without these foundational roles, the cybersecurity talent pipeline is at risk of collapsing, a problem that AI is likely to exacerbate across the broader tech industry.

Organizations must acknowledge this challenge and take proactive steps to:

- Redefine junior roles to focus on AI oversight and human-AI collaboration,
- Invest in upskilling programs to prepare future security professionals for AI-driven workflows, and
- Ensure that AI augments human expertise rather than replacing entry-level talent entirely.

The Future of SOCs: AI as a Partner, Not Just a Tool

Platforms like Kindo will proactively defend against threats, learn from every attack, adapt playbooks automatically, and continuously evolve, making future breaches increasingly difficult to execute.

This is the future everyone should be building toward, one where AI isn't just a tool but a strategic partner, evolving alongside the threats it defends against.

And the SOCs that embrace this future today will be the ones leading cybersecurity tomorrow.

Autonomous Infrastructure: The Backbone of Future SOCs

As AI continues to shape the cybersecurity landscape, a fundamental shift is happening; not just in how threats are detected, but in how infrastructure itself operates. Autonomous infrastructure is emerging as a critical pillar in security operations, reducing human dependencies, accelerating response times, and ensuring that SOCs can handle threats dynamically, without waiting for manual interventions.

What is Autonomous Infrastructure?

At its core, autonomous infrastructure integrates automation, artificial intelligence, and machine learning to create self-healing, self-scaling, and self-optimizing environments. In traditional SOCs, analysts spend hours manually correlating alerts, adjusting firewall rules, and configuring security tools. But what if this entire process could become self-managing? That's where autonomous infrastructure changes the game.

With AI first platforms like Kindo and WhiteRabbitNeo, SOC teams can move beyond manual tuning of security controls and log analysis. AI enhances detection algorithms using historical data, adjusts defenses based on real-time insights, and delivers actionable intelligence to analysts, allowing them to focus on high-value tasks. These platforms optimize performance through structured analysis and feedback, ensuring SOC operations remain efficient, adaptive, and responsive. As AI technology advances, the potential for continuous learning will further enhance SOC capabilities, enabling even greater adaptability and intelligence in the future.

How Autonomous Infrastructure Reshapes SOCs

The concept of autonomous infrastructure isn't just theoretical. It's already reshaping several key areas in SOCs:

1.   Incident Response Automation

Traditional SOCs rely on playbooks and manual escalation processes. With Kindo's AI-driven SecOps, security workflows are automated and refined through ongoing analysis of past incidents and user interactions. AI-driven agents analyze attack patterns, adjust firewall and endpoint rules based on real-time insights, and proactively contain threats before they escalate. By leveraging historical data and security policies rather than self-learning, Kindo ensures its optimizations align with the SOC's operational needs, enabling teams to respond at machine speed while maintaining full control over decision-making.

2.   Self-Optimizing Cloud Security (CSPM & CNAPP)

With hybrid cloud adoption increasing, SOCs struggle with cloud security posture management (CSPM) and cloud-native application protection (CNAPP). Autonomous infrastructure ensures that misconfigurations, policy violations, and vulnerabilities are detected and fixed proactively. Instead of waiting for an audit, the AI continuously evaluates cloud environments, enforcing real-time security policies.

3.   Threat Modeling and Attack Surface Reduction

With adversaries leveraging AI to scale attacks, security teams must anticipate and eliminate attack vectors before they're exploited. Kindo's AI-driven approach enables organizations to conduct automated attack simulations, model threats dynamically, and proactively remediate weaknesses before adversaries' strike.

4.   Infrastructure as Code (IaC) Security

SOCs increasingly rely on Infrastructure as Code (IaC) for cloud deployments. However, misconfigurations in IaC can introduce security gaps. Kindo ensures real-time analysis of IaC templates, identifying security issues before infrastructure is deployed. This proactive approach eliminates vulnerabilities at the source.

Why SOCs Need to Adapt Now

The adoption of autonomous infrastructure isn't just a competitive advantage, it's a necessity. The volume, velocity, and variety of cyber threats are outpacing traditional SOC capabilities. Without autonomous security layers, analysts are stuck in an endless cycle of manual investigation, patching, and remediation.

Using an AI first platform like Kindo and specialized cybersecurity and DevOps AI models like WhiteRabbitNeo enable SOCs to break this cycle by embedding AI-driven intelligence directly into security operations. This ensures continuous monitoring, predictive risk mitigation, and proactive response, without human bottlenecks.

The SOC of the future will not be defined by human-driven processes alone. It will be shaped by AI-driven infrastructure that learns, adapts, and evolves in real time. The combination of self-optimizing environments, AI-driven decision-making, and predictive automation ensures that security teams stay ahead of threats, not just responding to attacks, but preventing them before they happen.

Chapter Eight

Predictive Analytics for Proactive Cyber Defense

The Day Before the Attack

It started with a flicker, a moment so subtle that any traditional system would have ignored it.

At a major financial institution in the Gulf region, a senior network engineer was conducting a routine review of authentication logs. The bank, with operations across multiple markets in the region, handled high-value financial transactions, making it a prime target for cybercriminals.

That evening, an unusual login attempt had been detected from an executive's laptop.

The first attempt had failed. The second, just minutes later, had succeeded.

At first glance, it seemed harmless, possibly the executive had mistyped their password. The SOC team might have dismissed it as a minor issue. But their AI-powered predictive analytics system flagged it as a high-risk anomaly.

Not because of the failed login itself, but because it resembled patterns observed in recent cyberattacks targeting banks and financial institutions across the region.

Over the past six months, AI had analyzed hundreds of credential-based intrusions, revealing a recurring anomaly, subtle authentication irregularities that often signaled the early stages of credential-stuffing attacks.

This was one of those patterns.

Rather than waiting for an obvious breach, the SOC team launched an immediate investigation. They traced the source IP address, only to discover it had been spoofed, a telltale sign of an Advanced Persistent Threat attempting to move laterally within the network.

Without causing alarm, the AI system initiated automated countermeasures:

- It monitored the executive's account for any deviations in behavior.
- It flagged the device for an urgent security review.
- It restricted privileged access, preventing any unauthorized transactions.

By morning, when the attacker attempted to escalate privileges and gain deeper network access, they were already locked out.

A major security incident had been stopped before it could even begin.

This is the power of **predictive analytics**: turning hindsight into foresight, shifting security operations from reactive to proactive.

A Paradigm Shift in Cybersecurity

Predictive analytics has emerged as one of the most invaluable tools in the modern SOC arsenal. Every security professional knows that cyber threats never sleep. Attackers are constantly refining their tactics, making reactive security models obsolete. The only way to stay ahead is to predict where the next strike will occur.

Integrating predictive analytics into cybersecurity is not just an upgrade, it's a fundamental shift. Instead of waiting for an alert to fire, predictive models analyze historical data, evolving threat intelligence, and machine learning algorithms to forecast attack patterns. This allows SOC teams to foresee vulnerabilities before they are exploited, strengthening defenses in advance.

The goal is simple but powerful: **turn every incident into a lesson and every lesson into a shield.**

How Predictive Analytics Works

Predictive analytics builds on patterns, probabilities, and precision (not guesswork). It transforms raw data into actionable intelligence through:

- **Historical Data Analysis:** Reviewing past cyberattacks, breach attempts, and security logs to recognize recurring tactics, techniques, and procedures (TTPs).

- **Machine Learning Models:** AI-powered models continuously learn from new data, detecting patterns that humans might miss.

- **Behavioral Analytics:** Analyzing deviations from normal user and network behaviors to identify potential pre-attack indicators.

- **Threat Intelligence Integration:** Correlating internal security data with global threat intelligence feeds to anticipate emerging attack strategies.

- **Risk Scoring and Prioritization:** Assigning dynamic risk scores to assets, accounts, and systems based on real-time threat analysis.

Each new data point refines the accuracy of the predictions, making the system faster, sharper, and smarter with time.

Where Predictive Analytics Fits in the Modern SOC

1. Early Threat Detection

Traditional security models wait for a breach to occur before taking action. Predictive analytics eliminates this waiting period by identifying attack precursors, subtle indicators that often precede a full-scale intrusion.

For example, a SOC powered by predictive analytics might detect:

- Unusual access requests from a privileged user who has never logged in at 4 AM before.
- Increased failed login attempts across multiple departments, hinting at credential-stuffing attempts.
- A spike in data transfer requests to an external server, resembling data exfiltration tactics seen in past insider threats.

By recognizing these patterns early, security teams can intervene before damage occurs.

2. Dynamic Risk Assessment

Rather than treating all threats equally, predictive models prioritize risks dynamically. For instance, an AI-driven SOC doesn't just flag a failed login attempt, it cross-references it with:

- User behavior baselines (Has this user logged in from this location before?)

- Device reputation (Is this a known corporate device or an unfamiliar endpoint?)
- Threat intelligence feeds (Has this IP been associated with previous cyberattacks?)

If multiple red flags align, the system escalates the risk score, allowing SOC teams to act faster on the highest-risk incidents.

3. Proactive Defense Strategies

Instead of firefighting, predictive analytics enables preemptive defense measures, such as:

- Adjusting firewall rules dynamically based on predicted attack patterns.
- Increasing monitoring on at-risk assets before a breach attempt occurs.
- Preemptively isolating high-risk accounts showing anomalous behavior.

This reduces attack surface exposure and strengthens the overall security posture.

Kindo: Powering the Future of Predictive Cyber Defense

Kindo's AI-driven security platform brings the power of predictive analytics to your SOC. By leveraging real-time incident data and refining its models based on past interactions, Kindo helps SOC teams anticipate which assets, users, or systems may be at risk next.

With each detected anomaly, Kindo:

- Analyzes global attack trends to identify potential next targets.
- Correlates internal security logs with external threat intelligence to forecast emerging threats.
- Adapts dynamically to evolving tactics, ensuring no two attacks catch the SOC off guard.

This transforms security operations from passive response teams into intelligent, predictive defenders.

A Future Scenario: Predicting and Stopping a Supply Chain Attack

A global technology enterprise, heavily reliant on third-party vendors for software development and infrastructure support, leveraged Kindo's predictive analytics to secure its supply chain network.

Over a span of three months, the AI system detected early warning signs of a potential breach, including:

- Inconsistent login locations for an external vendor's account.
- Irregular data access patterns, suggesting account compromise.
- Failed authentication attempts from known attack vectors.

Instead of waiting for a breach, the SOC preemptively blocked access, conducted forensic analysis, and discovered the vendor's credentials had been stolen. This intervention prevented a supply chain attack that could have compromised thousands of connected enterprises.

The Future of Cybersecurity is Predictive

As cyber threats grow in speed and complexity, waiting to react is no longer an option. Predictive analytics equips SOCs with the foresight needed to anticipate and neutralize threats before they cause harm.

1. **From reactive to proactive** — no longer chasing threats but staying ahead of them.

2. **From alerts to intelligence** — understanding risks before they escalate.

3. **From defending to predicting** — transforming every lesson into a future shield.

As attackers leverage AI to automate their attacks, only AI-powered predictive analytics can match them in speed, intelligence, and adaptability.

In this new era of cybersecurity, success belongs to those who can see the threats of tomorrow — today.

AI-made problems need AI-made solutions. Stay ahead, predict, defend!

The Evolution of Predictive Analytics in Cybersecurity

Cybersecurity has always been a cat-and-mouse game, with attackers constantly evolving their tactics while defenders struggle to keep up. Traditional security tools could only react to threats after they were in motion, leaving organizations vulnerable to fast-moving, adaptive attacks.

Predictive analytics changed the game. Instead of waiting for clear signs of an attack, AI-driven models now detect subtle pre-attack behaviors, a sudden change in user activity, an unusual spike in network traffic, or patterns that mimic past breaches. These signals might seem harmless in isolation, but when analyzed across:

- Historical incidents,
- Threat intelligence,
- Internal behavior baselines,
- Open-source Intelligence (OSINT), and
- Real-time telemetry,

They reveal where the next attack is likely to happen.

Kindo takes this further, transforming fragmented data into early warning signals that help SOCs strengthen defenses with precision. It anticipates their next move, ensuring teams are ready before the first alarm even rings.

The best way to stop an attack? See it coming before it even begins.

The Role of Machine Learning and Data Science in Prediction

Predicting cyber threats isn't about using off-the-shelf AI, it's about training machines to think like attackers. Security data is messy, constantly changing, and full of noise. That's where machine learning comes in, identifying attack patterns before they unfold.

WhiteRabbitNeo enhances this by being an uncensored AI, unrestricted in analyzing real-world attack scenarios, evolving tactics, and adversarial techniques. Unlike traditional models that limit security research, it provides unfiltered insights to help SOCs anticipate even the most sophisticated threats.

By analyzing:

- historical breaches,
- infrastructure config changes / changes in code,
- failed logins,
- unusual file access, and
- endpoint activity,

AI models can recognize early warning signs, even when no traditional alert is triggered. A sudden spike in failed logins might seem harmless, but when combined with subtle shifts in user behavior, it could be the start of a credential-stuffing attack.

Kindo makes this intelligence actionable. Instead of waiting for an attack to become obvious, it detects pre-attack behaviors and alerts SOC teams while there's still time to act. The key isn't just having more data, it's having the right data, analyzed in real-time, turning the SOC into a threat predictor, not a threat responder.

Because in cybersecurity, seeing the future means stopping the breach before it happens.

Building a Predictive SOC: Practical Steps

Turning predictive analytics into a real-world advantage inside your SOC isn't about buying the fanciest AI tools or hiring a team of data scientists overnight. It's about building the right foundation, gradually embedding prediction into daily workflows, and creating a culture where data fuels decision-making at every level.

Here's how smart SOCs make that transition:

1. **Start with Data Quality**

   Predictive analytics is only as good as the data feeding the models. A predictive SOC ensures that all relevant telemetry (from network flows to user activity to endpoint logs) is collected, normalized, and enriched with context. No blind spots. No stale data. The better the data, the sharper the predictions.

2. **Enrich with Threat Intelligence**

   Internal data only tells half the story. To predict external threats, SOCs need continuous threat intelligence feeds: tracking adversary tactics, newly discovered vulnerabilities, and emerging attack campaigns. By combining internal patterns with external threat evolution, predictive analytics becomes more accurate and adaptive.

3. **Embed Machine Learning into the Workflow**

   Prediction can't live in isolation: it needs to flow directly into SOC processes. This means integrating predictive insights into the SIEM, SOAR, and incident management platforms analysts already use. Instead of treating prediction as a separate function, it becomes part of triage, investigation, and response.

This is exactly where Kindo fits into modern SOC evolution. By embedding predictive insights directly into response playbooks and detection workflows, Kindo helps spot potential future incidents tied to ongoing trends, feeding prediction directly into action.

4. **Build Feedback Loops**

A predictive SOC doesn't just predict once and move on. It learns from every incident. Every prediction (whether accurate or not) feeds back into the model, refining its ability to spot new threats. This continuous feedback loop keeps the models sharp, ensuring they evolve as fast as the threat landscape does.

5. **Shift from Static Playbooks to Adaptive Playbooks**

Traditional playbooks are one-size-fits-all. Predictive SOCs use adaptive playbooks that adjust dynamically based on predicted threat types, attacker behaviors, and evolving risk levels. Instead of treating every incident the same, the response adapts to what the prediction tells you about the adversary's intent.

6. **Cultivate a Predictive Mindset**

    Finally, technology alone isn't enough. Predictive SOCs need analysts who think like predictors: constantly asking what's next instead of just what happened. This cultural shift, from incident responders to risk forecasters, is what separates a predictive SOC from a reactive one.

When all these steps come together, the SOC transforms into a proactive intelligence hub, where machine learning anticipates threats, analysts act on predictive insights, and the entire security lifecycle moves from reactive to predictive.

Case Studies — Predictive Analytics in Action

Real-world incidents illustrate just how valuable predictive analytics has become for SOC teams. Here are a few standout cases where prediction made a real difference:

1. **SolarWinds Supply Chain Attack (2020)**

When the SolarWinds breach rocked the cybersecurity world, it wasn't just a story about advanced persistent threats (APTs), it was a wake-up call for predictive defenses. After the initial attack, organizations began using predictive analytics to track potential residual threats linked to compromised systems. Predictive models analyzed post-breach network behavior and compared it to pre-attack baselines, allowing analysts to spot dormant backdoors before they were exploited.

2. **MOVEit Transfer Data Breach (2023)**

Following the discovery of a zero-day vulnerability in MOVEit's secure file transfer system, predictive models were deployed to monitor similar software stacks, hunting for early signals of exploitation attempts. This proactive monitoring—powered by historical vulnerability patterns—allowed several organizations to patch and isolate systems before actual compromise occurred.

3. Microsoft Exchange ProxyShell Vulnerability (2022)

During the ProxyShell exploit wave, predictive analytics played a crucial role in vulnerability management. By analyzing historical data on Exchange-related exploits, predictive models helped SOC teams forecast which variants of ProxyShell were most likely to emerge next. This insight allowed for targeted patch prioritization, ensuring the most at-risk systems were hardened first.

These examples demonstrate that predictive analytics isn't just theoretical: it's practical, measurable, and essential in today's threat landscape. By continuously learning from historical events and anticipating what comes next, SOCs move from reacting to incidents to actively shaping their own defensive posture.

Who Benefits Most from Predictive Analytics?

The impact of predictive analytics extends across every industry—but certain sectors stand to gain the most:

- **Finance:** Monitoring transaction patterns for fraud and predicting future attack campaigns targeting payment systems.

- **Healthcare:** Detecting unusual access to medical records and forecasting data breaches aimed at personal health information (PHI).

- **Government:** Anticipating state-sponsored campaigns aimed at critical infrastructure or sensitive government data.

- **Service Providers:** Security vendors themselves use predictive analytics to enrich their threat intelligence platforms, offering clients preemptive guidance on emerging threats.

With an AI first platform Kindo acting as both an incident response engine and a predictive advisor, security teams across these industries gain not only faster response capabilities but also a constantly evolving threat radar tailored to their own unique environments.

Predictive Analytics — More Than Just Prediction

At its core, predictive analytics in cybersecurity isn't just about forecasting, it's about enabling the 3 Ps of Threat Intelligence:

- **Proactive:** Actively hunting for threats before they escalate.
- **Predictive:** Using historical data, threat intelligence, and behavioral patterns to estimate future attacks.
- **Preventive:** Taking action based on predictions to close vulnerabilities, adjust controls, and limit risk before threats materialize.

SOCs that adopt predictive analytics move from passive observation to active foresight, allowing them to shift from firefighting mode to risk shaping mode, where security is continuously adapting ahead of threats.

This predictive power gets applied in several key areas:

1. **Threat Intelligence and Anomaly Detection:**

   Machine learning models ingest historical incidents, network telemetry, user behaviors, and open-source intelligence (OSINT) to identify anomalies that fit pre-attack patterns. Even zero-day attacks show some precursors, and predictive analytics can detect those weak signals.

2. Risk Assessment and Prioritization:

Predictive models don't just detect threats — they also assess risk exposure by correlating internal vulnerabilities with external attack trends. This helps teams prioritize security investments, focusing limited resources on the most likely threats.

3. Automated Response and Threat Mitigation:

Kindo uses predictive analytics not only to flag potential incidents, but also to trigger automated response actions in SOAR systems. For example, if behavior linked to lateral movement is detected, predictive systems can automatically isolate segments of the network before the attacker progresses.

All of this happens in real time, embedded into the SOC's normal operating rhythm, so analysts benefit from prediction without disruption.

Ethical and Privacy Considerations in Predictive Analytics

Predictive analytics works because it consumes a lot of data: from internal logs to third-party feeds to behavioral metadata. But this reliance on big data comes with serious ethical responsibilities.

- Are you collecting only necessary data?
- Are you anonymizing data where possible?
- Are your predictions explainable and defensible, or are they a black box?

These aren't just regulatory checkboxes; they are essential for trust. Whether you're under GDPR, ISO27001, NCA ECC, or UAE IA, predictive analytics must comply with strict data minimization and purpose limitation rules. Platforms like Kindo are designed with these principles in mind, ensuring all predictive insights are fully auditable, so your team can show each what decision was made and why.

Benefits and Challenges

Benefits:

- **Reduced Detection Time:** Predictive models spot threats earlier by recognizing pre-incident behavior.

- **Smarter Resource Allocation:** SOC resources focus on high-likelihood threats, increasing efficiency.
- **Faster Response:** Pre-attack warning means controls can activate earlier, reducing dwell time and damage.
- **Continuous Learning:** Every incident feeds the prediction engine, making future predictions sharper.

Challenges:

- **Data Quality Matters:** Predictive power is only as good as the data feeding the models.
- **Model Drift:** Attack techniques change, so models must be constantly retrained.
- **Explainability Gaps:** Predictive systems must show their work, or they lose analyst trust.
- **False Positives:** Overly aggressive prediction models can create noise, overwhelming analysts instead of helping them.

Implementing Predictive Analytics — Process Flow

Here's how mature SOCs bring predictive analytics to life:

1. **Data Collection:** Historical breaches, incident logs, threat intelligence, user behavior — the full stack.

2. **Data Analysis:** Applying machine learning and statistical analysis to find correlations and patterns.

3. **Pattern Recognition:** Identifying recurring pre-attack behaviors — the breadcrumbs attackers leave behind.

4. **Threat Modeling:** Creating what-if scenarios, simulating how future attacks might unfold.

5. **Decision Support:** Using those models to prioritize risks, update controls, and guide proactive actions.

The predictive process becomes a living part of daily SOC life, constantly refining itself with new data and outcomes.

Looking Ahead: From Reactive to Predictive to Autonomous Cyber Defense

Predictive analytics is just the beginning. The real transformation lies in autonomous security: where SOCs don't just detect or predict threats but actively defend, adapt, and evolve without waiting for human intervention.

With AI-driven optimization at machine speed, platforms like Kindo and WhiteRabbitNeo are enhancing SOC workflows with intelligent, data-driven defense mechanisms. WhiteRabbitNeo, with its broad analytical capabilities, strengthens predictive defenses by analyzing real-world attack strategies, while Kindo automates proactive responses based on structured insights and past interactions. This ensures security teams don't just react faster but stay ahead of evolving threats. The future SOC won't be measured by how fast incidents are closed, but by how many never happen in the first place. Security won't be about catching threats; it will be about outpacing and outmaneuvering them before they even materialize.

This is the new baseline. The SOCs that embrace this shift today will be the ones defining cyber resilience tomorrow.

Of course, for AI-driven security to be truly effective, it must also be operationally efficient. In the next chapter, we'll explore how AI optimizes SOC workflows, reduces analyst fatigue, and makes security teams faster and smarter than ever before.

Chapter Nine

Operational Efficiencies Through AI

By now, you've likely seen the relevance of AI across nearly every industry. But when it comes to cybersecurity, especially in building efficient SOC operations, the value of AI goes beyond hype—it becomes essential. To understand why, you first need to answer one simple question: Why do you need AI in your SOC?

The answer is not about replacing your team or cutting costs. It's about enabling your team to focus on what humans do best: strategy, threat hunting, and creative problem-solving, while AI handles the repetitive, time-sensitive, and data-heavy tasks.

Despite the benefits, many organizations still hesitate to fully adopt AI. This hesitation is understandable, especially with concerns about third-party tools collecting excessive data or acting as hidden backdoors. These concerns are valid, but ignoring AI entirely is no longer an option. The real risk isn't in using AI: it's in trying to secure modern, complex environments without it.

That's why choosing trusted solutions that comply with regional and global regulations is critical. Platforms like Kindo are designed to balance automation with transparency and control, ensuring you gain efficiency without sacrificing privacy, compliance, or human oversight. AI doesn't have to mean giving up control, it should mean enhancing control through better visibility, faster action, and smarter decisions.

Think about your own daily schedule: meetings to attend, deals to close, partnerships to build. Every minute spent on manual incident handling is time you can't spend on business growth. AI changes that equation. With automation, your SOC becomes an autonomous security engine, freeing your team to focus on high-value tasks without compromising your cyber defenses.

Now imagine your cybersecurity posture without automation. SOC analysts glued to their screens 24/7, chasing every minor alert, manually pulling logs from different systems just to piece together a timeline: it's neither sustainable nor scalable. And the cost? Not just in salaries or overtime, but in missed opportunities, analyst burnout, and slower response times that amplify risk.

AI removes these bottlenecks, enabling your SOC to scale up operational efficiency without expanding headcount. With AI-driven platforms like Kindo, you can focus on growing your business while knowing your SOC is working at machine speed to keep threats at bay.

Automating Routine SOC Tasks

In any SOC, the bulk of analyst time is spent on repetitive, low-value tasks. Alert triage, log correlation, creating incident reports, assigning severity levels, manually updating tickets, escalating to higher levels, and others. These are necessary steps, but they rarely require deep analytical thinking. Yet they consume a disproportionate amount of time, leaving analysts with little bandwidth for proactive threat hunting or strategic risk management.

AI dramatically reduces this operational drag by taking over the repetitive grunt work, allowing analysts to focus on higher-order decision-making. Modern SOC platforms already embed AI-driven automation directly into these workflows:

- **Automated Alert Triage:** AI evaluates incoming alerts against historical incidents, threat intelligence feeds, and behavior baselines to prioritize which ones need immediate attention.

- **Log Correlation:** Instead of requiring analysts to pivot across multiple tools, AI automatically correlates data across endpoints, networks, and cloud platforms, delivering a unified incident narrative.

- **Incident Reporting:** AI generates pre-filled reports, automatically documenting root cause analysis, impacted assets, recommended actions, and supporting artifacts.

- **Ticket Management:** Use Kindo to integrate with ITSM platforms and can create, enrich, and update incident tickets within ITSM platforms like ServiceNow or Jira, ensuring incident tracking is always up to date without manual input.

This level of automation amplifies the effectiveness. Analysts move from being manual process executors to strategic decision-makers. Their time is spent analyzing, not assembling.

With platforms like Kindo, automation isn't just a feature but it's part of the fabric of how incidents are handled. Every detection automatically triggers contextual workflows, with pre-filled fields, attached artifacts, and suggested next steps. Analysts don't start with a blank screen: they start with actionable intelligence, already prepared by the system. And the best part? These efficiencies compound over time, making the entire security operation smarter with every incident handled.

AI-Driven Incident Correlation and Contextual Enrichment

One of the biggest time sinks in any SOC is incident correlation: the process of connecting isolated alerts into a single, cohesive story. In traditional SOCs, analysts must manually pull logs from different systems, cross-reference timestamps, match IP addresses, and try to reconstruct the timeline of what happened. This is painstaking work, especially during multi-stage attacks where the breadcrumbs are scattered across endpoints, networks, cloud services, and user behavior logs.

AI transforms this process into an automated narrative builder. When an alert triggers, AI doesn't just present the isolated event, but it correlates related signals across the environment. This means:

- Matching the alert to historical incidents with similar patterns.
- Pulling in relevant artifacts from endpoints, network traffic, identity logs, and even threat intelligence feeds.
- Building an attack timeline automatically, showing how the event started, what was affected, and what potential next steps the attacker might take.

Instead of analysts manually chasing clues, they receive a pre-built incident timeline that has already been enriched with technical context, risk scoring, and initial response recommendations. This reduces time-to-understanding by orders of magnitude, allowing analysts to spend their time making decisions instead of gathering data.

With Kindo, correlation goes beyond simply stitching together logs. Its autonomous agents analyze past incidents, refining pattern recognition and data correlation to enhance detection accuracy. As your SOC processes more incidents,

Kindo optimizes its correlation engine, improving operational efficiency without requiring manual tuning.

The real power of AI-driven correlation is that it allows the SOC to understand the full scope of an attack instantly, rather than piecing it together over hours or even days. This accelerates containment and ensures that related threats don't get overlooked: especially in stealthy, slow-moving attacks, where individual events may appear harmless in isolation but signal danger when viewed as part of a broader pattern.

The result is clear:

- Faster understanding,
- Faster decisions,
- Faster resolution,

All with less manual workload. That's what operational efficiency looks like in an AI-enabled SOC.

Reducing False Positives and Alert Fatigue

A friend of mine, an L1 SOC analyst, once told me something that stuck: "The only email I got from my L2 team last year simply said, 'False positive.'"

That's it. One email.

Every day, he and his team escalated alerts, only to be told they weren't real threats. Again, and again. But what if just one of them wasn't a false positive? What if the attack was hiding in plain sight, lost in the noise?

This is the brutal reality of alert fatigue, SOC teams drowning in endless notifications, most of which turn out to be nothing. Over time, analysts stop paying attention, increasing the risk of missing the one threat that actually matters.

This is where AI changes everything. Kindo and WhiteRabbitNeo cut through the noise by not just scoring alerts but understanding them in context. Instead of dumping every event onto analysts, Kindo enriches, correlates, and prioritizes threats based on real-world attack patterns, asset importance, and historical intelligence. WhiteRabbitNeo, with its uncensored AI capabilities, ensures nothing is overlooked, spotting subtle adversary tactics that traditional models might filter out.

Now, instead of getting hundreds of meaningless alerts, analysts get fewer but highly relevant cases: fully investigated, with decision-ready insights. No more guesswork. No more blind escalations.

Because in cybersecurity, one false positive too many can mean missing the real attack. And no SOC can afford that.

AI in Reporting and Compliance Automation

Nobody likes getting that dreaded email from the GRC team or an auditor, the one that politely asks for proof of compliance, incident reports, or security documentation. It's never a quick request. It's a time-consuming hunt through SIEM logs, playbooks, and case notes, trying to reconstruct every detail of an incident that happened weeks or months ago.

For many SOC analysts, compliance reporting feels like a second job, one filled with endless spreadsheets, manual cross-checks, and late-night searches for missing artifacts. And let's be honest, no one signs up for cybersecurity to do paperwork.

This is where AI-driven automation changes everything. Instead of analysts digging for evidence, AI automatically builds the story. Every alert, response action, and root cause analysis are logged, enriched, and structured into a report in real-time.

By the time an incident is closed, AI has already:

- Created a detailed timeline from detection to resolution.
- Identified key indicators of compromise (IoCs) and attack patterns.
- Documented all automated and manual response actions taken.
- Linked the incident to related cases and historical attack data.
- Provided compliance-ready summaries tailored to frameworks like GDPR, PCI DSS, HIPAA, SOC2, NIST, CMCC, NCA ECC, UAE IA, ISO 27001, SAMA CSF or others.

With Kindo, this process happens within the SOC workflow. Analysts don't have to rebuild reports from scratch or chase missing data, they simply validate and finalize AI-generated reports before submission. Audit readiness is no longer a last-minute scramble, it's a continuous state.

Beyond compliance, AI also helps SOC leaders spot trends, identifying recurring attack types, vulnerabilities, and response inefficiencies, without spending hours crunching spreadsheets.

The result? Faster reports, smoother audits, and more time for analysts to focus on real security work. And the next time that email from GRC lands in your inbox? You'll already have the answers ready.

AI-Enhanced Knowledge Management

It's 7 AM, and an L1 SOC analyst is staring at an alert that looks eerily familiar. He's almost certain they've seen this attack pattern before — but the analyst who handled the last case? Fast asleep after pulling a night shift.

Hesitantly, he dials the number. The groggy voice on the other end mutters something about "Check the old tickets" before hanging up. Desperate for answers, the analyst starts digging through disconnected logs, emails, and Slack messages, hoping to find anything useful.

Then comes the next nightmare — the SOC manager walks in. "Why wasn't this documented last time?" he demands, rubbing his tired eyes. Frustrated, the team scrambles to piece together knowledge that should have been at their fingertips.

This is the reality of poor knowledge management in SOCs: critical insights locked in analysts' heads, buried in emails, or lost when experienced team members leave.

In any SOC, knowledge is one of the most valuable assets, but also one of the hardest to manage effectively. Every incident, every investigation, every remediation action holds lessons that could strengthen future response. Yet, in most SOCs, this knowledge gets trapped in individual minds, scattered across emails, and buried in incident tickets. Institutional knowledge walks out the door every time an experienced analyst leaves.

AI changes this dynamic by automating knowledge capture and retrieval, turning every incident/ alert / event into a teachable moment and every response into a reusable playbook component. AI-powered platforms automatically record key artifacts, decisions, and lessons learned from each incident, indexing them into searchable knowledge repositories, removing manual documentation processes.

This turns the SOC's collective experience into a living, breathing knowledge base, available to every analyst in real time. When a new incident occurs, analysts can immediately see if similar incidents happened in the past, how they were handled, what worked, and what didn't. AI can even recommend relevant past cases based on the context of the current incident, accelerating analysis and avoiding repeated mistakes.

This process is built directly into the response workflow of Kindo. Every playbook execution, every manual action taken, and every analysis comment gets captured and indexed automatically, enriching both the individual case record and the broader SOC knowledge pool. Analysts no longer have to rely on memory or dig through disconnected systems: the answers are surfaced for them, in context, when they need them most.

This isn't just about efficiency, it's about resilience. When knowledge is institutional rather than individual, the SOC becomes less vulnerable to turnover and operates at a consistently high level even when new analysts join the team. AI-enhanced knowledge management ensures that every incident makes the SOC smarter, feeding a continuous cycle of learning, adapting, and improving.

In the end, a SOC is only as strong as what it remembers and applies. AI turns that memory into a practical, operational advantage, ensuring that every past battle strengthens the defenses for the next one.

AI-Driven Threat Containment and Firewall Change Assistance with Kindo

Imagine this: A SOC analyst identifies a suspicious IP communicating with critical assets. The immediate recommendation? Block the IP. But here's where things stall.

- The analyst submits a firewall change request.
- The request moves through approval workflows, waiting for manual review.
- If it's after hours, the firewall update doesn't happen until the next business day.

By the time the change is implemented, the threat may have already moved on, or worse—breached more systems.

Traditionally, SOCs are responsible for detecting threats, while firewall policy changes fall under IT operations or network security teams. This division creates inefficiencies, leaving security gaps open longer than necessary.

Kindo's Role in AI-Driven Threat Containment and Firewall Change Assistance

Kindo integrates with IT ticketing systems (e.g., Jira, ServiceNow, Linear) to automate firewall change proposals based on SOC alerts. Instead of waiting for ITOps to manually analyze and apply rules, Kindo:

1. **Automates the Ticketing Process** – When a SOC alert recommends a firewall rule change, Kindo automatically creates a ticket with pre-validated security logic.

2. **Generates AI-Driven Change Recommendations** – Instead of requiring ITOps to manually determine the best rule updates, Kindo analyzes the request and proposes rule changes based on the organization's firewall configuration.

3. **Provides Risk Analysis and Justification** – Kindo assesses the risk of the proposed change and highlights potential vulnerabilities before execution.

4. **Improves IT Security Workflow** – By automating low-risk rule changes, Kindo reduces the burden on IT teams and accelerates security enforcement.

5. **Integrates with Firewall Management Solutions** – Works alongside existing firewall management tools like FireMon to streamline and validate rule adjustments.

6. **Ensures Compliance and Documentation** – Every recommendation is logged for auditability, ensuring traceability and compliance with security frameworks such as NIST, NCA ECC, and ISO 27001.

This approach turns firewall change management into a faster, AI-assisted workflow, ensuring that security recommendations from SOCs are executed promptly and efficiently.

How to Automate Firewall Change Proposals

Step 1: Triggering AI Automation Based on SOC Alerts

- Kindo integrates with ticketing systems like Jira, ServiceNow, or Linear.
- A firewall-related request in a ticket triggers Kindo's AI agent, identifying the required rule changes.

Step 2: AI-Driven Analysis and Configuration Review

- Kindo's White Rabbit Neo AI model analyzes the ticket and cross-references the organization's firewall configuration.

- The AI assesses the best rule updates needed to address the request.

- Example: If the request says, "Allow external SFTP traffic," Kindo reviews existing firewall rules and suggests precise changes.

Step 3: Automated Proposal Submission

- Kindo adds a comment to the ticket with AI-generated firewall rule recommendations.

- IT teams receive a pre-validated rule change proposal, ready for approval and execution.

Step 4: Execution and Logging

- If pre-approved, low-risk rules can be automatically applied.

- All actions are logged within Kindo and the ticketing system for transparency and compliance.

Use Case: Reducing Bottlenecks in Firewall Rule Updates

Scenario: Faster Threat Containment Through AI-Driven Firewall Recommendations

Challenge:

A SOC detects an active reconnaissance attempt from a known malicious IP address. The SOC analyst needs the IP blocked immediately, but it's 2 AM, and the IT operations team won't be available until morning.

Traditional Process:

The SOC analyst submits a firewall rule change request through a ticketing system. With no available ITOps team overnight, the request remains unprocessed until their shift begins. This delay allows attackers more time to exploit vulnerabilities before any action is taken.

Solution with Kindo:

The Kindo agent detects the firewall change request and triggers an AI-driven response. AI analyzes the request, reviews existing firewall configurations, and suggests precise rule changes. A comment is automatically added to the ticket, providing the SOC and ITOps teams with actionable firewall rules. If the change is pre-approved, Kindo can execute the modification instantly, eliminating unnecessary delays.

Outcome:

Threats are contained instantly, reducing dwell time and minimizing security risks. Overnight security gaps caused by manual approval delays are eliminated, ensuring faster incident response. *Collaboration between SOC and ITOps improves*, streamlining firewall rule management and enhancing overall security efficiency.

Benefits of AI-Driven Firewall Change Assistance

1. Reducing SOC-to-ITOps Delays

SOC-driven security updates shouldn't be stuck in overnight queues. Automating firewall change proposals eliminates IT workload bottlenecks, ensuring threats are blocked without unnecessary delays.

2. AI-Enhanced Security Workflows

Manual entry errors can lead to misconfigurations. AI-generated, risk-validated firewall recommendations help IT teams make precise, informed decisions, improving security without added complexity.

3. Ensuring Compliance and Auditability

Every firewall change is fully documented for audits, ensuring alignment with ISO 27001, NCA ECC, and PCI DSS. Security teams get full visibility without compliance headaches.

4. Streamlining Firewall Policy Adjustments

Firewall rules tend to get messy over time. AI dynamically analyzes configurations, suggests precise rule updates, and reduces redundancy, optimizing security policies for efficiency and effectiveness.

Best Practices for Implementing AI in Firewall Management

1. Define Pre-Approved AI-Driven Firewall Change Policies

Not all firewall changes should be automated. Establish clear policies to differentiate between AI-handled updates and those requiring manual approval. AI-driven risk scoring ensures low-risk changes happen instantly, while high-risk requests get the necessary scrutiny.

2. Create an AI Feedback Loop

AI gets smarter with experience. Continuously train AI models using IT and SOC feedback to refine rule suggestions and improve accuracy. Automation workflows evolve based on real-world security incidents, making the system more adaptive over time.

3. Implement Role-Based Access Controls (RBAC)

AI can propose changes, but execution needs control. Restrict rule enforcement to authorized security personnel, ensuring that critical firewall updates still require human oversight. This balance enhances security while maintaining accountability.

4. Regular Security Audits and Compliance Checks

Even AI needs a second set of eyes. Monitor change logs to detect misconfigurations and refine AI-generated policy recommendations in response to emerging threats. Continuous audits ensure compliance stays aligned with evolving security frameworks.

With Kindo, SOC teams can automate firewall rule change proposals, reducing dependency on manual IT approvals and minimizing security delays. By integrating AI-driven recommendations into ticketing workflows, organizations can:

- Improve incident response time.
- Reduce security risks caused by delayed firewall changes.
- Ensure compliance and auditability of every firewall modification.

This AI-driven approach makes SOC-driven security recommendations more actionable, efficient, and scalable, helping organizations stay ahead of modern cyber threats while maintaining seamless IT governance.

Measuring Operational Efficiency Gains with AI

Every security investment eventually comes down to one question: what difference did it make? AI in the SOC is no different. For all its potential, AI adoption must be measurable, showing clear improvements in efficiency, accuracy, and overall operational performance. Without tangible metrics, even the smartest automation can end up seen as just another tool, instead of the strategic enabler it should be.

The good news is that operational efficiency gains from AI are highly measurable, across several dimensions:

1. **Mean Time to Detect (MTTD)**

   AI dramatically reduces the time needed to detect real threats by filtering noise, correlating events automatically, and enriching alerts with context upfront. Comparing MTTD before and after AI implementation is one of the clearest ways to demonstrate its impact.

2. **Mean Time to Respond (MTTR)**

   By automating repetitive tasks, from ticket creation to artifact correlation to report generation: AI reduces the hands-on time analysts need to fully resolve incidents. Faster detection combined with faster response workflows leads to measurable MTTR reductions.

3. **Analyst Productivity**

   With AI taking over lower-level work, each analyst can handle more incidents per shift, without a corresponding increase in fatigue or error rates. This is especially visible in alert triage and routine incident handling.

4. False Positive Rate

One of AI's most immediate impacts is reducing noise by suppressing low-risk, irrelevant alerts. Tracking the percentage of alerts closed as false positives before and after AI implementation paints a clear picture of its filtering power.

5. Knowledge Utilization

AI-enhanced knowledge management means analysts spend less time reinventing the wheel and more time applying lessons already learned. Measuring the reuse rate of historical incidents, playbooks, and lessons learned gives direct insight into how well the SOC leverages institutional knowledge.

With Kindo, these metrics are automatically tracked and visualized, giving SOC leaders clear, continuous visibility into how AI enhances day-to-day performance. This helps justify AI investments and allows leaders to tune processes further, continuously refining the balance between automation and human oversight.

Challenges in Automating Routine Tasks

While automation brings enormous benefits, transitioning from manual to automated workflows isn't always smooth. Legacy processes, deeply ingrained habits, and even internal resistance can slow down automation initiatives. Every SOC has its own workflows, tailored over years of trial and error. Trying to replace those processes overnight with automated alternatives can disrupt operations if not managed carefully.

The key is to approach automation incrementally: starting with the most repetitive, high-volume tasks like alert triage, basic correlation, and routine reporting. Gradually expanding automation, while giving analysts time to adapt and provide feedback, helps strike the right balance between automation and human oversight.

Another challenge is ensuring automation itself doesn't become a vulnerability. Automated workflows (if misconfigured) could accidentally suppress critical alerts, isolate key systems, or take overly aggressive actions without human input. This is why platforms like Kindo embed

223

human-in-the-loop checkpoints for sensitive actions, ensuring that critical decisions always have analyst oversight.

Business Process Automation (BPA) and Robotic Process Automation (RPA) in SOCs

SOCs increasingly turn to BPA and RPA to drive operational efficiency. BPA focuses on end-to-end process automation, streamlining multi-step workflows across tools and teams. RPA, on the other hand, automates specific, repetitive tasks: mimicking manual actions like data entry, log retrieval, or ticket updates.

By integrating BPA and RPA with SIEM, SOAR, and ITSM platforms, SOCs create seamless, touchless workflows. Alerts flow directly into automated playbooks, enrichment data is fetched instantly, and tickets update themselves as incidents progress. Analysts become conductors rather than manual processors, focusing their time on high-impact analysis and decision-making.

With platforms like Kindo, AI controlled BPA and RPA is not bolted on later, it is built into the core incident response engine, ensuring every process benefits from speed, consistency, and reduced manual effort.

Enhancing SOC Analyst Productivity and Focus

SOC analysts juggle an overwhelming number of alerts every day. Between triage, investigation, documentation, and reporting, their workload leaves little time for proactive hunting or skill development. AI alleviates this pressure by automating routine tasks, but productivity gains only happen if analysts trust the automation and understand how to work with it.

That's why AI-driven SOCs invest in training programs that teach analysts not just how to use AI tools, but how to collaborate with them. Analysts learn to interpret AI-generated risk scores, validate automated enrichment, and provide feedback to improve models over time. This human-AI partnership ensures that automation enhances productivity without disempowering analysts.

Training SOC Analysts for AI-Driven Environments

AI is only as effective as the people using it. Analysts need training that covers:

- Understanding how AI models work, so they can trust the outputs.

225

- Learning how to tune and refine AI workflows to fit the organization's threat landscape.
- Practicing when to override automation, especially for nuanced threats that require human intuition.
- Developing skills in proactive threat hunting, model validation, and feedback loops, ensuring AI continues to learn and adapt in alignment with real-world threats.

This blend of technical training, operational adaptation, and mindset shift transforms analysts from manual responders to strategic overseers, making the SOC smarter with every incident handled.

The Role of AI in Offensive Security and SOC Operations

SOCs are primarily responsible for monitoring, detecting, and responding to security threats, while offensive security teams, such as red teams, penetration testers, and bug bounty hunters, proactively identify vulnerabilities before attackers exploit them.

Traditionally, SOC teams react to threats, but integrating AI-driven offensive security tools allows proactive threat identification and mitigation before incidents occur.

With Kindo and WhiteRabbitNeo, AI-powered automation enhances offensive security operations by:

- Analyzing and explaining code and config changes before they create a problem
- Vulnerability scan reports (e.g., Nmap) with clear explanations of what reported issues mean and how to resolve them
- Identifying CVEs based on service versions found in scans
- Generating proof-of-concept (PoC) attack scripts for given vulnerabilities
- Providing remediation guidance to mitigate discovered risks.
- Automating report generation for SOC and security teams

This capability benefits SOC teams by integrating offensive security insights into their workflows, allowing faster response times, improved threat intelligence, and preemptive remediation before real attacks occur.

Kindo's Role in AI-Driven Offensive Security

How It Works:

1. **Scanning and Data Collection**
   - A penetration tester or security analyst runs an Nmap scan on a target system.
   - The scan results list open services, software versions, and configurations.
   - Kindo automatically imports the scan results and analyzes them for vulnerabilities.

2. **Vulnerability Identification and CVE Mapping**
   - Kindo's AI model matches detected services and versions to known vulnerabilities from sources like the National Vulnerability Database (NVD) and MITRE CVE database.
   - It then summarizes each CVE, explaining its risk level and exploitability and how to mitigate.

3. **Generating Attack Proof-of-Concepts**
   - Kindo can construct an attack scenario based on an identified vulnerability.
   - Using WhiteRabbitNeo, it writes PoC exploit code in multiple programming languages.
   - The AI ensures the attack simulation is aligned with ethical hacking and red team methodologies.

4. **Providing Remediation and Security Recommendations**
   - Alongside offensive testing, Kindo generates remediation steps to mitigate vulnerabilities.
   - SOC analysts and IT security teams receive detailed guidance on patching, configuration changes, or access control improvements.

5. **Automated Report Generation**
   - Kindo automates security report creation, summarizing the vulnerabilities, exploitability, and mitigation steps.
   - This allows SOC teams to quickly act on offensive security findings, reducing the attack surface before real attackers exploit it.

Use Case: Enhancing SOC Intelligence with AI-Powered Offensive Security

Scenario: AI-Assisted Vulnerability Identification & Exploitation Simulation

Challenge:

A SOC team is responsible for proactively identifying security weaknesses before attackers do. However, manually analyzing scan reports, mapping vulnerabilities, and developing PoC exploits is a time-consuming process that can take hours or even days. This delay in security improvements leaves organizations vulnerable to potential threats. Furthermore, the traditional approach requires significant manual effort, making it prone to human error and inefficiencies.

Traditional Process:

In a conventional workflow, the security team begins by running an Nmap scan to identify active services and open ports within the network. Analysts then manually search CVE databases to determine whether the detected services are associated with known vulnerabilities. If a vulnerability is found, security experts develop proof-of-concept (PoC) exploit scripts by hand to validate the risk. Once validated, findings are documented in reports, which are then submitted for remediation actions. This entire process is labor-intensive, repetitive, and highly susceptible to oversight or misclassification, reducing the effectiveness of security operations.

Solution with Kindo:

By integrating Kindo's AI-powered capabilities, SOC teams can significantly streamline this process. Nmap scan results are automatically processed by Kindo's AI, which rapidly maps detected services to known CVEs, eliminating the need for manual lookup. AI-driven automation further accelerates security testing by generating PoC exploit code, allowing ethical validation of vulnerabilities in a controlled environment. Additionally, Kindo provides suggested remediation steps and their priority, enabling SOC teams to address vulnerabilities more efficiently. Automated reporting ensures that findings are documented with accuracy and consistency, reducing the burden of manual reporting while enhancing operational efficiency.

Outcome:

By leveraging Kindo's AI-driven offensive security capabilities, SOC teams experience a significant reduction in the time required for vulnerability analysis and reporting. The integration of AI enhances accuracy, allowing for faster and more informed threat intelligence processing within SOC workflows. Additionally, collaboration between offensive security teams and SOC analysts becomes more seamless, fostering a more proactive approach to cybersecurity.

Benefits of AI-Driven Offensive Security for SOCs

1. Faster Threat Discovery and Exploit Testing

- AI automates vulnerability lookup and PoC generation, reducing analysis time.
- SOC teams receive immediate insights into exploitable weaknesses.

2. Better Collaboration Between Red Teams and SOC Analysts

- AI helps bridge the gap between offensive security and SOC monitoring.

- Findings are integrated into real-time threat intelligence workflows.

3. Improved Security Response Through AI-Generated Remediation

- AI provides detailed security fixes, guiding IT and security teams.
- Helps prevent attacks before real-world exploitation occurs.

4. Automated Compliance and Reporting

- AI-driven documentation streamlines security reporting.
- Ensures compliance with frameworks like ISO 27001, NIST, and PCI DSS.

Best Practices for Implementing AI-Augmented Offensive Security in SOCs

1. Integrate Offensive Security into SOC Workflows

- Use AI first tools like Kindo to proactively identify security gaps.

- Ensure SOC teams act on vulnerability insights before threats escalate.

2. Automate CVE Analysis and Exploit Generation

- Leverage AI to map vulnerabilities to PoC exploits.
- Reduce manual efforts by using automated testing recommendations.

3. Use AI to Enhance Threat Intelligence

- Combine offensive security insights with SOC threat detection.
- AI-generated reports should be shared with IT teams for immediate fixes.

4. Maintain Ethical and Legal Guidelines for AI-Driven Offensive Security

- Ensure AI-generated PoC exploits are used responsibly.
- Offensive security should align with ethical hacking and penetration testing policies.

AI-driven offensive security is not just about attack simulations, but about enhancing SOC threat intelligence, vulnerability remediation, and proactive defense strategies. By integrating Kindo's AI-driven vulnerability analysis and exploit generation, SOC teams can:

- Identify and remediate vulnerabilities faster.
- Automate PoC exploit creation and security recommendations.
- Improve collaboration between red teams and SOC analysts.

This AI-powered approach ensures proactive security, reducing the attack surface before threats become real breaches. AI is not just an assistant in SOCs; it's an enabler for a more secure, intelligent cybersecurity strategy.

Redefining SOC Efficiency with Kindo and WhiteRabbitNeo

Security teams today are overwhelmed, not just by cyber threats but by the operational inefficiencies that come with managing disparate security tools, responding to alerts, and manually piecing together the cybersecurity puzzle. The reality is that traditional SOC workflows are too slow, fragmented, and reactive.

Kindo is built to change this. It orchestrates security operations holistically, allowing security teams to shift from reactive firefighting to proactive threat management. It does this through six fundamental pillars:

1. Unified Multi-Modal Approach

Security infrastructures often consist of multiple tools; SIEM, EDR, NDR, XDR, SOAR, CSPM, IAM, and more, each operating in isolation. Kindo acts as the intelligence layer that stitches all these pieces together, ensuring security teams have a single, unified operational view instead of jumping between dashboards.

Use Case: Incident Response – Instead of analysts manually correlating logs across SIEMs and EDRs, Kindo auto-correlates alerts and provides enriched threat narratives, allowing teams to act in minutes rather than hours.

2. Flexible AI Model Integration with WhiteRabbitNeo

Unlike many solutions that force enterprises into a single AI model, Kindo's architecture supports multiple AI models, including its flagship WhiteRabbitNeo. This flexibility allows teams to select the best AI for the job, optimizing detection accuracy and operational efficiency.

Use Case: Threat Intelligence & RCA (Root Cause Analysis) – Security teams can dynamically swap AI models depending on the nature of the incident. WhiteRabbitNeo powers intelligence gathering, ensuring teams work with real-time, actionable threat insights instead of outdated indicators.

3. Seamless RCA & IAM Security

Identity and Access Management (IAM) is one of the biggest operational bottlenecks in cybersecurity. Kindo automates IAM security by seamlessly integrating with enterprise authentication systems (e.g., Okta, SAML, Active Directory), ensuring security teams enforce strict access control without compromising agility.

Use Case: Automated Role-Based Access Control (RBAC) – Instead of engineers manually tracing permission errors, Kindo auto-detects misconfigurations, reducing IAM troubleshooting from hours to minutes.

4. Self-Managed Deployment for Data Sovereignty

Many enterprises hesitate to embrace AI-driven SOC solutions due to compliance concerns over data sovereignty. Kindo solves this by offering a self-managed deployment option, allowing enterprises to run Kindo in their own cloud or fully on premise to maintain full control over data privacy and infrastructure security. Easy to deploy and operate world class AI models are now offered open source allowing the entire AI stack to be kept fully private.

Use Case: CSPM & Cloud Security – Organizations can deploy Kindo and state of the art open-source AI models within on-premises environments or private clouds, ensuring sensitive security data never leaves their controlled perimeter.

Yes, you read it right, Kindo can be deployed on-premises, allowing organizations to maintain full control over their data and AI infrastructure. This deployment flexibility ensures that sensitive security data remains within the organization's-controlled environment, addressing compliance and data sovereignty concerns. This capability aligns with the growing trend of organizations seeking more control over their IT infrastructure due to AI and security concerns, leading to a shift towards on-premises solutions.

5. AI-First Governance & Compliance Infrastructure

AI-driven security doesn't just mean faster threat detection — it also requires transparency, compliance, and full auditability. Kindo was designed with governance in mind, ensuring SOCs meet industry-specific compliance frameworks such as GDPR, HIPAA, and SOC2.

Use Case: Audit Logging & Governance – Every AI-driven decision made within Kindo is fully auditable, ensuring enterprises maintain compliance with regulatory and internal risk policies.

6. Enterprise-Grade Data Loss Prevention (DLP)

While many AI-powered security platforms lack built-in Data Loss Prevention (DLP), Kindo integrates robust DLP features into AI workflows, preventing accidental data exposure or breaches.

Use Case: Automated Data Tokenization – Before sending sensitive data to AI models, Kindo automatically redacts sensitive information, ensuring privacy-first security operations.

Case Studies — Successful Human-Machine Teams

Real-world examples showcase the power of AI-human collaboration:

- **Emaar Hospitality Group:** Uses AI chatbots to handle routine guest interactions, freeing human agents to deliver personalized service. Behind the scenes, predictive analytics anticipates service demands, ensuring staffing and resources are always optimized.

- **Dubai International Airport (DXB):** Combines AI-driven passenger flow analytics with real-time operational adjustments, reducing congestion and improving passenger satisfaction. AI not only detects potential bottlenecks but recommends operational changes to prevent them.

- **Lulu Group:** Applies AI personalization engines to deliver customized shopping experiences, while AI also monitors site behavior for fraud detection and content filtering—ensuring security and personalization happen side by side.

- **Aldar Properties:** Enhances property search and matching using AI, creating personalized recommendations based on user preferences, while also using AI-driven visual guides and virtual tours to improve the overall customer experience.

- **Abu Dhabi Investment Authority (ADIA):** Leverages AI for risk modeling and investment analysis, while using AI chatbots for investor queries. This blend of operational efficiency and customer experience enhancement has become a blueprint for AI-driven operational transformation.

These cases all show a common truth: AI works best when humans and machines collaborate, each playing to their strengths: automation for speed and scale, human intuition for nuance and creativity.

Efficiency is Resilience

In cybersecurity, efficiency is not a luxury: it's a survival skill. Every hour recovered from manual grunt work is an hour that can be spent on proactive threat hunting, improving detection rules, or strengthening the organization's security posture.

AI's role in the SOC isn't to replace people; it's to amplify them, giving analysts the time, tools, and intelligence they need to succeed. When repetitive tasks are automated, incident data is instantly enriched, and historical knowledge is served up at the moment it's needed, the SOC evolves from reactive firefighting to proactive mastery.

This is the true value of AI in operations. It's about embedding resilience into the very fabric of how the SOC works. A resilient SOC is the one where people, processes, and technology form a seamless learning loop, growing smarter with every incident. That's what operational efficiency means in the AI-powered SOC.

But with all this power comes a new responsibility. AI in cybersecurity must be ethical, explainable, and transparent. Automation should never be a black box: decisions must be justified, privacy must be safeguarded, and AI must operate within legal and ethical boundaries.

In the next chapter, we explore the ethical and legal implications of AI in SOCs: because efficiency without ethics isn't just a risk; it's a vulnerability.

Chapter Ten

Ethical and Legal Implications of AI in SOCs

It started with a simple question during a compliance audit at a leading SOC services provider in the Gulf region:

"Can you explain why the AI flagged this employee at one of your biggest banking clients as a security risk?"

The room fell silent. The AI system had detected anomalous behavior from a bank employee and had automatically triggered an account lockout as a security measure. While this proactive response seemed effective, the real challenge arose when the auditors demanded an explanation. The SOC analysts reviewed the alert logs, but there was no clear, interpretable reason for why the AI had identified this particular employee as a risk.

The auditors weren't satisfied with a vague response like "the AI detected a threat." They needed specifics. What data had been used to classify the behavior as anomalous? What risk thresholds had been crossed? Which decision-making factors had led to the system's automated action? However, neither the security team nor the AI engineers could provide a definitive answer. The model's complex algorithms, trained on vast behavioral datasets, lacked transparency in their decision-making process.

The issue wasn't whether the AI was wrong, the employee's behavior could have indeed been suspicious. The real problem was that no one could prove it was right. And in a region increasingly focused on compliance with international cybersecurity frameworks, failing to justify an AI-driven decision posed a serious regulatory and ethical challenge. The auditors made it clear: unless the SOC could demonstrate clear, explainable reasoning behind AI-generated security decisions, the legitimacy of such actions (and the company's compliance standing) would remain in question.

This incident underscored a critical issue facing modern SOCs: AI can enhance security, but without transparency and accountability, it can also introduce serious legal and ethical risks, especially when dealing with financial institutions where regulatory scrutiny is at its highest.

Legal and Regulatory Compliance: Navigating the Global and Regional Maze

From the NCA ECC and DCC in Saudi Arabia to UAE's NESA and IA standards, the regulatory landscape across the Gulf is evolving fast—often faster than technology itself. AI-driven SOCs must not only comply with cybersecurity regulations but also demonstrate explainability when it comes to how decisions are made. Privacy laws, data residency rules (especially in GCC's government sectors), and sector-specific mandates create a complex web of obligations for every SOC leader to navigate.

At the international level, compliance extends to GDPR for European operations, HIPAA for healthcare, and ISO 27001 for general information security governance. In finance, PCI DSS adds additional layers of responsibility. Each of these regulations demands clear data handling practices, rigorous access controls, and in many cases, explicit user consent when AI systems process personal data.

Kindo is designed with regulatory alignment in mind. It helps organizations navigate this maze by embedding compliance monitoring directly into its AI workflows, automatically documenting which data sources were accessed, what processing took place, and ensuring every action taken is audit ready. This reduces not only compliance overhead but also the risk of regulatory penalties if an incident is later scrutinized.

Because in cybersecurity, being right isn't enough: you need to be able to prove it.

Privacy, Data Protection, and Ethical AI Use

AI-enabled SOCs rely heavily on massive data ingestion: the richer the data, the better the models—but with this comes a direct collision with privacy rights and data protection laws. Security monitoring often captures employee activity, personal identifiers, and communications metadata, raising critical questions: How much data is too much? Who has access? Where is it stored?

In regions like the GCC, where data sovereignty is a major concern, SOCs must be careful not only about what data is collected, but also where that data is processed and stored.

Cloud-based AI solutions that move data across borders can trigger compliance red flags, making data residency a critical factor in AI adoption.

Beyond legal risks, AI introduces ethical blind spots. When an AI model labels a user's behavior as risky, it's not just a technical decision—it's a judgment call that could impact careers, reputations, and system access. Without transparency, AI can turn into an unquestioned black box, leaving SOC teams unable to explain or challenge its decisions.

This is where Kindo takes a different approach. Every AI-driven decision is traceable, with a full audit trail detailing what data was used, what historical incidents influenced the decision, and why a particular action was recommended. This ensures AI doesn't just dictate actions, but provides clear, accountable insights that analysts can review, question, and refine.

Because trust in AI doesn't come from its intelligence: it comes from its transparency.

The Fine Line — Censorship vs Non-Censorship in AI Models

There's a delicate ethical boundary between responsible filtering and outright censorship when AI governs what analysts can see, generate, or explore. This is especially relevant when AI models assist in knowledge retrieval, advisory generation, or proof-of-concept (PoC) creation during investigations.

Consider two different AI platforms:

- WhiteRabbitNeo, which allows analysts to generate proof-of-concepts for vulnerabilities, enabling deep technical testing.
- Claude, which restricts PoC generation, limiting its usefulness in technical forensics.

This raises a fundamental question: Should AI systems censor technical knowledge in the name of ethical risk management, or should they empower analysts with unrestricted access, trusting human oversight to guide responsible use?

Both approaches have risks:

- Too much freedom, and AI could facilitate misuse or unintended harm.
- Too many restrictions, and AI could cripple investigative capabilities, slowing down critical incident response.

The balance lies in contextual governance. AI in SOCs must recognize who is using the system, for what purpose, and within what operational guardrails. Kindo addresses this by ensuring role-based access and contextual advisory: a Tier 1 analyst might see simplified advisory notes, while a senior incident responder can unlock more technical, exploratory content for deep-dive forensics.

This ensures responsibility without unnecessary censorship, preserving the SOC's technical agility while aligning with legal and ethical obligations. AI doesn't need to act as a gatekeeper, it should act as a context-aware advisor, guiding analysts rather than blindly restricting them.

This debate isn't just about ethics; it's about operational practicality. During real-time incident response, when threats evolve by the minute, analysts need all possible tools at their disposal. If AI restricts testing exploitability or replicating attack chains, it risks slowing containment or leaving gaps in understanding.

However, unrestricted AI access carries risks, particularly for less experienced analysts. The same AI that generates a legitimate PoC for defensive testing could also produce weaponized code if prompts are poorly framed, potentially leading to misuse or internal security risks. This is where context-aware AI governance is critical, ensuring:

1. Access matches skill level: Junior analysts see high-level guidance, while senior responders access deeper insights.
2. Every sensitive action is logged, explained, and, if necessary, reviewed post-incident.
3. Regulatory frameworks, like NCA ECC (Saudi Arabia), UAE IA, GDPR, NIST are factored into AI-based decision-making.

Ultimately, how a SOC governs AI-driven content generation reflects its security culture. Highly mature SOCs with strong governance may allow full transparency, trusting human oversight for ethical decisions. Emerging SOCs or those in heavily regulated industries may prefer tighter AI controls, prioritizing risk reduction over speed.

The key takeaway? *Censorship isn't binary: it's a spectrum.* Every organization must find the right balance based on risk appetite, regulatory exposure, and operational maturity.

For those interested in exploring this topic further, I've written another book, "**AI and Us: The Ethical Choices,**" which dives deeper into the broader ethical dilemmas of AI, censorship, and responsible decision-making. Readers can find it online and continue the conversation about where we should draw the line in AI governance.

Bias, Explainability, and the Role of Human Oversight

One of the most frequently overlooked challenges in AI-enabled SOCs is bias in decision-making. Every AI model is only as objective as the data it's trained on. If historical incidents show a bias toward over-flagging certain behaviors (for example, unusual working hours being treated as inherently suspicious) the AI will inherit and perpetuate that bias. In diverse global workforces, particularly across GCC organizations operating in multiple time zones, such biases can directly lead to false positives targeting legitimate work patterns.

Explainability becomes the counterbalance to bias. Analysts must be able to see not just what decision the AI made, but also why it made that decision. What signals triggered the risk score? What historical cases influenced this classification? Without that transparency, AI quickly becomes a black box, eroding analyst trust and undermining operational confidence.

This is why Kindo embeds explainability directly into every AI-driven action, ensuring that every flag, every recommendation, and every automated response is traceable back to its data sources and logic flow. Analysts don't have to take the AI's word for it: they see the underlying reasoning and can challenge or refine it if necessary. This creates a healthy feedback loop, where human expertise continuously tunes the AI, reducing bias drift over time.

Human oversight isn't just a safety net: it's a critical design principle in ethical AI deployment. AI can accelerate decisions, but those decisions still need to reflect organizational values, risk tolerance, and regulatory context.

Every SOC needs clearly defined handoff points, where AI flags and humans decide, ensuring that high impact decisions, such as deactivating user accounts, isolating critical systems, or triggering external notifications, always retain a human stamp of approval.

This partnership between transparent AI and accountable human oversight is what separates responsible automation from blind automation. It preserves both speed and accountability, ensuring that efficiency gains never come at the expense of ethical responsibility.

Legal Liability and Accountability in AI-Driven SOCs

The introduction of AI into SOC operations creates a new layer of legal complexity. In a traditional SOC, responsibility for decision-making rests squarely with the human analyst, every action they take is directly attributable to their judgment. When AI steps in to automate or even recommend actions, the question becomes: Who is ultimately accountable when something goes wrong?

If AI recommends isolating a critical production server and that action causes a major service outage, who carries the blame: the analyst who trusted the AI's recommendation, the

SOC manager who deployed the AI, or the vendor who built the AI system? This is no longer a hypothetical debate; as AI becomes operationally embedded into incident response workflows, these accountability questions will increasingly land in courtrooms and regulatory hearings.

Regulations already place clear responsibility on organizations to demonstrate due diligence when using AI for data processing or security decision-making. In practice, this means SOCs must:

- Maintain detailed audit trails showing how AI arrived at each decision.
- Demonstrate that AI systems were properly trained, tested, and governed before deployment.
- Ensure that analysts retain the final authority for high-impact actions, even if AI initiates recommendations.
- Regularly audit AI performance for bias, error rates, and false positives, proving that the system is fit for purpose under real-world conditions.

This is where platforms like Kindo offer a valuable advantage, by embedding full lifecycle traceability into its AI-driven workflows, it allows SOC leaders to produce audit-ready documentation showing how every incident was handled, what data shaped each decision, and where human oversight came into play. This ensures that accountability is clear at every step, protecting both the organization and individual analysts from ambiguity in case of post-incident reviews or regulatory scrutiny.

Legal accountability doesn't mean avoiding AI entirely: it means deploying AI with care, governance, and continuous oversight. In this sense, trustworthy AI isn't just a technical capability, it's a compliance necessity. And the SOCs that understand this will not only move faster operationally but also stand stronger legally when challenged.

Transparency Expectations from Regulators and Customers

Transparency has become a defining expectation for SOCs deploying AI. This isn't just about regulatory compliance: it's about building trust with both external regulators and internal stakeholders. When AI influences or directly automates security decisions, stakeholders; from board members to auditors to business owners, want to know how those decisions are made.

For regulators, transparency is essential for proving due diligence. Under frameworks like NCA ECC, GDPR, and ISO 27001, organizations must demonstrate that AI-enhanced security processes follow established governance principles, including:

- Documented workflows showing where and how AI is used.
- Explainability mechanisms proving why a particular action was recommended or taken.
- Role-based access controls ensure that AI decisions align with corporate risk posture.
- Regular audit trails confirming the AI system is monitored, tuned, and evaluated for bias and performance.

For internal stakeholders (especially non-technical leadership) transparency helps bridge the knowledge gap between technical operations and business risk management. Executives need to understand how AI decisions affect business continuity, regulatory compliance, and reputational risk. They need confidence that AI isn't introducing invisible risks into the security process.

This is why Kindo, along with other leading AI platforms, builds explainability directly into its user interface. Every AI-generated recommendation comes with a plain-language explanation showing the underlying evidence, risk factors considered, and historical patterns detected. This level of transparency doesn't just help analysts, it helps build executive and regulatory confidence that AI is acting as a responsible partner, not a wildcard.

Transparency isn't just good governance: it's operational insurance. In the event of a regulatory review or legal dispute, SOCs with clear documentation of every AI action are far better positioned to demonstrate compliance and defend their decisions. This makes transparency a practical necessity, not just an ethical preference.

Ethical AI Governance Frameworks

Deploying AI in the SOC without a clear governance framework is like handing over the keys to a powerful engine without knowing how fast it can go or where the brakes are. Ethical governance ensures that AI operates within defined boundaries, aligned not only with legal requirements but also with the organization's values, risk tolerance, and cultural expectations.

Many organizations adopt established AI governance frameworks to guide this process. These frameworks emphasize core principles such as:

- **Fairness:** AI must make decisions consistently, without bias toward specific user groups, regions, or behaviors.
- **Transparency:** Every decision made by AI must be explainable, showing what data was used, what logic applied, and what past cases influenced the recommendation.
- **Privacy Preservation:** AI must minimize data collection, anonymize wherever possible, and always respect the data subject's rights.
- **Accountability:** AI is never an independent actor — responsibility always rests with human operators, who must oversee, validate, and take ownership of AI-assisted decisions.
- **Continuous Monitoring:** AI models must undergo ongoing performance reviews to

detect drift, rising false positive rates, or evolving biases.

With Kindo, these principles are embedded into daily SOC operations. Every action taken by Kindo's autonomous agents is fully auditable, every recommendation is explainable, and every piece of data processed is traceable back to its source and its purpose. This ensures that ethical governance is not just a policy document, but a living process embedded into how the SOC functions day-to-day.

Beyond frameworks, governance committees play a critical role in AI oversight. These committees bring together security leadership, compliance officers, legal counsel, and business executives, ensuring that AI-enabled processes align with both operational realities and regulatory expectations. Regular AI risk reviews, cross-departmental discussions, and clear escalation paths for AI-related concerns help maintain a strong ethical foundation.

Ethical governance doesn't slow down innovation: it enables responsible innovation. By defining clear boundaries, governance allows SOC teams to leverage AI confidently, knowing they have both the freedom to innovate and the guardrails to stay safe. It's this balance (between agility and control) that defines mature, ethical AI adoption in cybersecurity.

Building Trust in AI: Overcoming Transparency and Reliability Concerns

AI in cybersecurity promises efficiency and precision, but trust issues arise when it misfires — flagging too many false positives, missing real threats, or making opaque decisions that analysts struggle to interpret. Without transparency, AI risks becoming more of a burden than a benefit.

A major concern is over-reliance on automation. If AI floods analysts with false alerts, it wastes valuable time; if it fails to flag real threats, the consequences can be catastrophic. AI must strike a balance, reducing noise while maintaining accuracy.

To address this, modern SOCs prioritize explainability. Instead of black-box decisions, AI must show how alerts are classified and why threats are prioritized. Kindo ensures all AI-driven actions are logged, auditable, and refined with human feedback, minimizing false positives while staying adaptive to evolving threats.

Another objection is autonomous decision-making without visibility. Security teams won't fully trust AI unless they can verify its logic. Kindo solves for this by offering explainable AI, so every step includes:

- Data sources used
- Reasoning behind threat prioritization
- Confidence level of the AI's assessment
- Recommendations for further validation

This transparency keeps analysts in control while leveraging AI's machine-speed intelligence. The most successful SOCs won't replace humans with AI but they'll empower them, ensuring AI is an explainable, accountable, and continuously improving partner, not an opaque black box.

Preparing for AI Audits and Post-Incident Investigations

AI-enabled SOCs must be audit-ready at all times. Whether facing a regulatory audit, an internal compliance review, or a post-incident forensic investigation, the burden of proof rests with the organization to demonstrate that AI systems were used ethically, legally, and responsibly. This means keeping clear, complete records of:

- What data was processed by AI systems.

- What models were used, and how they were trained and validated.

- What decisions the AI influenced, and what supporting evidence was used.

- Which human approvals (if any) were required before high-impact actions were taken.

- What governance controls were in place to detect bias, drift, or misuse.

These records form the compliance backbone for AI audits. The goal isn't just to prove that AI worked: it's to demonstrate that AI worked within the boundaries defined by law, policy, and ethics. Kindo offers a practical advantage, automatically capturing a full forensic audit trail for every AI action, ensuring that every detection, decision, and response is traceable and explainable.

Post-incident investigations add an extra layer of complexity. After a significant security breach, regulators, customers, and even the board may demand a detailed reconstruction of what happened: including how AI systems contributed to detection, escalation, and response. If the AI missed key signals or made biased decisions, the SOC will need to account for those gaps, showing what corrective actions were taken to improve future performance.

To prepare for this, mature SOCs conduct regular AI tabletop exercises, simulating audit scenarios where they walk through the full AI decision lifecycle for past incidents. These exercises ensure the SOC team is ready to explain not just the outcome, but the entire process: from data ingestion to model inference to response execution.

In the end, AI audits are not just about compliance: they are about building confidence. The more clearly a SOC can show how AI operates, why it makes certain recommendations, and what oversight mechanisms exist, the stronger the case for responsible AI adoption. This transparency doesn't just satisfy regulators, it builds trust with customers, partners, and leadership, proving that the SOC is not just fast and efficient, but also accountable and ethically grounded.

Regional and Global Compliance — Walking the Tightrope

Every AI-enhanced SOC operating in the Gulf faces a dual compliance challenge — adhering to local regulatory frameworks while ensuring global best practices are also met, especially for international businesses. Regulators like UAE's

NESA and IA, Saudi Arabia's NCA (ECC and DCC), and Bahrain's Personal Data Protection Law all demand clarity in how AI processes, stores, and analyzes sensitive data: particularly for governmental or financial institutions where data residency rules are strict.

At the same time, multinational companies operating in the region also fall under the umbrella of global regulations such as GDPR, HIPAA, PCI DSS, and ISO 27001. This forces SOC teams to design AI processes that respect both local and international laws simultaneously requiring data localization strategies, clear documentation of processing activities, and cross-border data handling transparency.

Kindo addresses this challenge by embedding compliance-aware automation directly into its workflows. As it processes incident data, Kindo tags data sources, classifies regulatory relevance (local vs. global), and logs every data transfer event, ensuring a real-time compliance record that can be instantly retrieved for regulatory reviews. This proactive approach enables compliance by design, not by afterthought but a critical capability for modern AI-powered SOCs striving for operational readiness.

Ethical Use of AI—Beyond Compliance

Legal compliance defines the minimum acceptable standard, but truly ethical AI in SOCs goes further. Ethical use means ensuring the AI respects organizational values, cultural sensitivities, and workforce trust. This is particularly sensitive in markets with high immigration, such as the U.S., where diverse workforces bring varying perspectives on privacy and fairness, and in the GCC, where expats from multiple cultures, religions, and professional backgrounds work side by side. AI-driven monitoring and decision-making must be fair, unbiased, and explainable, ensuring no group is disproportionately impacted by automated risk assessments or behavioral profiling.

Ethical AI isn't just about following rules: it's about building trust. Organizations that embed transparency, fairness, and accountability into their AI-powered SOCs will not only meet compliance requirements but also foster a security culture where AI is seen as a trusted ally, not an unchecked authority.

Ethical AI use means:

- **Fairness:** AI decisions must apply equally to all users, without reinforcing cultural, gender, or ethnic biases (again as under Ethical AI Governance Frameworks).

- **Transparency:** Users whose activities are flagged must have the right to understand why they were flagged and have the ability to challenge decisions if necessary. (again, as under Ethical AI Governance Frameworks).

- **Purpose Limitation:** Data collected for security must never be reused for non-security purposes, such as HR performance evaluations or productivity scoring.

- **Cultural Awareness:** In highly diverse environments, AI's understanding of "normal" vs. "anomalous" behavior must account for cultural work variations — for example, work schedules during Ramadan or region-specific collaboration patterns.

The ethical compass of the SOC doesn't belong to technology alone: it must be owned by leadership, baked into policies, and actively enforced through governance committees. AI supports this only if it's configured to reflect these values, and platforms like Kindo play a key role by ensuring customizable risk scoring models that align with each organization's unique risk culture, not just generic global templates.

Managing Workforce Impact—The Human Side of AI Adoption

One of the most overlooked ethical dimensions of introducing AI into the SOC is how it affects the people working there. While AI reduces workload and handles repetitive tasks, it can also spark fear; fear of job displacement, fear of deskilling, or fear of being constantly watched by algorithms scoring every decision.

A responsible SOC doesn't just deploy AI, it actively manages the human transition, ensuring:

- **Proactive Communication:** SOC leaders must explain why AI is being introduced, what problems it solves, and how it will support analysts rather than replace them.
- **Training and Upskilling:** Analysts need training not only to operate AI tools, but also to understand AI logic so they can confidently validate and challenge AI decisions.

- **Clear Role Definitions:** As AI takes over triage, correlation, and reporting, human roles shift toward higher-value work—proactive threat hunting, hypothesis-driven investigations, and advisory roles within the organization.

- **Psychological Safety:** Analysts must feel safe disagreeing with AI outputs or flagging questionable recommendations, knowing that their input is valued—not punished.

Kindo, as a solution designed for collaborative human-AI interaction, stands out. It automates decisions while maintaining transparency, invites human review, and refines its performance based on human feedback. The result is a shared intelligence loop, where analysts feel empowered by AI, not displaced by it.

Preparing for the Fine Line—Censorship vs. Empowerment

As covered earlier, the line between censorship and responsible guidance in AI-powered SOCs is razor-thin. Whether it's about restricting access to exploit development tools or filtering advisory content AI provides to analysts, this fine line must be defined and governed upfront.

The goal is not to dumb down the SOC, it's to ensure that AI enhances productivity while reinforcing ethical boundaries. This means:

- Avoiding over-censorship that limits necessary technical creativity in incident response.
- Avoiding under-censorship that could allow AI tools to generate content that violates organizational, legal, or cultural norms.
- Embedding contextual filters so sensitive tools and data are only accessible to the right roles at the right time, with clear accountability logs for every access event.

In practical terms, this means Kindo (as an example) could dynamically adjust what PoC generation capabilities are available depending on the severity of the incident, the analyst's role, and the regulatory context of the environment being defended.

Censorship, when applied blindly, undermines operational efficiency. When applied intelligently, it becomes responsible access control — protecting the organization, the analyst, and the mission at the same time.

Responsible AI is the Foundation of Trust

As AI becomes a permanent force inside the modern SOC, efficiency alone isn't enough. True success comes from trust — trust from analysts who rely on AI's insights, trust from leadership who must defend those decisions, and trust from regulators who expect every action to stand up to ethical and legal scrutiny.

This trust doesn't come automatically just because the technology is advanced. It must be deliberately built into the system: through explainability, complete auditability, and strong governance processes that actively monitor for bias, drift, and misuse. AI is only as effective as the controls wrapped around it and the culture of accountability that drives its use.

The strongest SOCs in the future won't be defined by how much they automate or how fast their AI runs, but by how seamlessly humans and AI collaborate, with full transparency. Every action in Kindo autonomous agents take is fully traceable, every recommendation is explainable in plain language, and every data source used is clearly documented. With Kindo, the SOC becomes more accountable, more predictable, and more aligned with regulatory expectations.

This is what responsible AI looks like: not slowing down progress but making progress sustainable. Kindo enhances human judgment, but accountability always remains with the people in the SOC. Ethical AI is not just about compliance, it's about creating a security culture that values transparency as much as speed.

With that foundation of responsible AI in place, the next logical step is understanding how AI and human analysts complement each other. Because even in the most advanced SOC, AI doesn't work alone. The next chapter explores exactly that: how Kindo and your analysts become a team, blending human intuition and creativity with machine speed and scale to create a truly resilient, future-proof SOC.

Chapter Eleven

Human-Machine Collaboration in SOCs

The incident review meeting had started, and the SOC manager wasn't happy.

"We had all the signs—why did it take six hours to escalate?" he asked, flipping through the timeline on the screen.

The L1 analyst sighed. "Because the logs didn't look connected at first. We only saw the pattern later."

The AI specialist in the room chimed in. "Actually, the system flagged a correlation three hours in, but it wasn't acted on."

Silence.

That's when it hit the team: the SOC wasn't missing threats because of bad AI or bad analysts, it was missing threats because they weren't fully working together. The AI had spotted something, but the analysts didn't trust it enough to take immediate action. The humans saw activity, but they were too busy with low-priority alerts to connect the dots in time. It wasn't a technology problem; it was a collaboration problem.

The Symbiotic Relationship of AI and Analysts

Modern SOCs don't function on humans alone or AI alone — they rely on both working in sync. AI excels at speed, scale, and pattern recognition, while analysts provide intuition, context, and strategic oversight. But collaboration isn't automatic; it needs to be built with trust, explainability, and seamless workflows.

- Machines process millions of events in real time, detecting hidden correlations.
- Humans bring judgment, experience, and the ability to challenge AI's assumptions.
- The key is alignment! Ensuring both works as one, rather than in silos.

Kindo: The Digital Analyst That Evolves with You fits naturally into this collaborative model, not just as an automation tool but as a trusted digital teammate. Every human decision (accepting, rejecting, or refining AI insights) contributes to a growing knowledge base, enhancing the system's ability to refine its responses. Over time, Kindo doesn't just detect threats: it adapts to your SOC's response patterns, aligning with its unique risk landscape.

The Future of AI-Augmented Security Teams

At the end of the meeting, the SOC manager looked at his team.

"The AI did its job. We hesitated. Next time, we trust the system and act faster."

And that's what true human-machine collaboration looks like, not just better automation, but a smarter SOC where AI and analysts evolve together.

Defining Roles in Human-Machine Collaboration

For human-machine collaboration to thrive inside SOC, there must be absolute clarity on who does what. Ambiguity creates confusion, and confusion leads to missed alerts, overreactions, and broken workflows. Effective collaboration depends on clearly defined roles, ensuring that both the human team and the AI system know their place in the operational flow.

Humans excel at contextual understanding, creative problem-solving, and strategic thinking. They spot patterns that don't fit neatly into models, interpret subtle cultural or geopolitical context, and apply intuition that comes from years of frontline experience. Machines, on the other hand, are relentlessly fast, processing terabytes of data across endpoints, networks, and cloud environments in seconds. They never get tired, they never miss a log, and they learn directly from every incident handled.

In a well-orchestrated SOC, the AI handles detection, correlation, enrichment, and initial triage, surfacing only the incidents that matter. The human analyst validates the context, applies strategic judgment, and drives containment and remediation actions. In this sense, the human is the decision-maker, while the machine becomes the ultimate data gatherer, analyzer, and advisor.

With Kindo, this role division goes beyond theory—it is seamlessly integrated into the workflow. Kindo's autonomous agents operate in the background, enriching every alert with historical context, relevant threat intelligence, and suggested next steps. By the time an analyst reviews an incident, it is pre-assembled, pre-scored, and pre-documented, enabling analysts to focus on decision-making rather than data collection.

This division of labor does not diminish the role of the analyst, it elevates it. Analysts become decision architects, using their skills to ask better questions, test creative hypotheses, and improve detection logic, rather than playing data janitor. The result is a faster, smarter, and more engaged SOC team, where people trust the AI to handle the heavy lifting, and the AI trusts the people to provide the critical human judgment AI can never replicate.

Building Trust Between Analysts and AI

The success of human-machine collaboration doesn't come from technology alone, it comes from trust. If analysts don't trust the AI, they will ignore its recommendations, double-check every action manually, and ultimately turn automation into dead weight. On the other hand, blindly trusting AI without understanding how it works can introduce dangerous risks, allowing biased, incomplete, or incorrect decisions to slip through.

This is why transparency and explainability are the foundations of AI trust in the SOC. Analysts need to see not just what the AI recommends, but also why? What triggered the alert? What data was analyzed? What historical patterns shaped the risk score? Without this context, analysts are forced to either trust blindly or distrust entirely: neither of which leads to effective collaboration.

Kindo addresses this trust gap by ensuring every recommendation comes with a full explanation: a clear, readable audit trail showing how the AI reached its conclusion. Analysts aren't asked to trust Kindo because it's fast, they trust it because they understand its reasoning, and they have the final say on every critical action. This transparency doesn't just build confidence in the tool, it turns analysts into active participants in training the AI itself.

Trust also grows through consistency. When AI handles routine incidents the same way every time, analysts see that the system is reliable. When AI surfaces only the high-risk, meaningful alerts, analysts see that it's smart enough to filter the noise. Over time, this reliable performance creates a sense of partnership, where the analyst feels that the AI has their back, not just throwing more data onto their desk.

SOC leaders play a crucial role in shaping the culture of trust. They need to set the tone: making it clear that AI is here to assist, not replace; that questioning AI is healthy, not defiant; and that every interaction between analyst and AI makes the whole system smarter for the future. When leaders reinforce this collaborative mindset, analysts no longer see AI as a threat; they see it as an extension of their own capabilities.

Continuous Learning—How AI and Humans Sharpen Each Other

Effective human-machine collaboration goes beyond clear roles and mutual trust. The real power lies in a continuous learning loop, where humans and AI enhance each other with every incident, every decision, and every investigation. This dynamic evolution keeps the SOC adaptive, ensuring it stays ahead of attackers rather than just keeping up.

Machines refine their understanding from every analyst action—whether an event is escalated, an incident's severity is adjusted, or a response action is modified. This feedback strengthens AI-driven detection, correlation, and prioritization, aligning responses more closely with the organization's unique environment, culture, and risk appetite.

But learning isn't one-sided. Analysts also gain deeper insights from AI by reviewing correlation patterns, automated timelines, and enriched incident context. This shared intelligence enhances proactive threat hunting, purple teaming exercises, and detection engineering, fostering a SOC that not only responds faster but understands threats on a deeper level.

With Kindo, refinement and optimization are embedded into the platform. Every analyst action—whether accepting, rejecting, or modifying recommendations—enhances detection logic and playbook automation, ensuring that SOC workflows evolve to reflect operational realities rather than just generic automation rules.

This mutual learning also helps bridge the cybersecurity talent gap. New analysts, who may lack deep experience, benefit from Kindo's embedded intelligence, gaining insights into incident correlation and recommended actions.

Meanwhile, senior analysts enhance Kindo's precision by applying domain expertise to fine-tune detection logic. This collaborative mentoring effect transforms the SOC into a learning ecosystem, where AI accelerates skill-building, and human expertise guides AI-driven decisions.

Ultimately, the goal is to build a SOC that learns and evolves, not just from external threat intelligence, but from its own people and tools working in unison. This is the essence of resilient security operations, where humans and AI grow smarter together with every incident faced and every lesson learned.

Training SOC Analysts for AI-Driven Environments

Human-machine collaboration works best when analysts understand how AI fits into their workflows, technically and also philosophically. SOC analysts need to know that AI is not replacing their role but elevating it. This requires a deliberate and ongoing training program, designed to build technical competence, operational confidence, and cultural alignment with the AI-powered SOC.

Training should begin with demystifying the AI itself. Analysts should understand how AI processes data, how it detects patterns, how risk scores are calculated, and how machine learning models evolve over time. This basic understanding turns AI from a mysterious black box into a trusted teammate whose behavior analysts can predict and influence.

From there, training must become practical and hands-on, focusing on how to interact with AI inside the daily workflow. Analysts should practice:

- Reviewing AI-generated incident timelines and enriched artifacts.
- Providing feedback (approving, rejecting, or modifying AI recommendations) understanding how that feedback influences future detections.
- Investigating how AI decisions were made, tracing back to data sources, historical patterns, and enrichment layers.

Kindo simplifies this training journey by making explainability a built-in feature. Every action taken by Kindo's autonomous agents is linked to a clear reasoning trail, so analysts don't need to reverse-engineer decisions. They can simply click, review, and understand, seeing exactly why a particular risk score was applied or a specific playbook was triggered. This accelerates learning while building confidence.

Beyond technical training, SOC leadership must also emphasize the cultural side of collaboration, encouraging analysts to challenge AI decisions when necessary, knowing that human oversight is a core part of responsible automation. Analysts must feel empowered to trust their instincts, even if AI presents a different recommendation, ensuring that AI enhances human judgment without overriding it.

Ultimately, training for AI-driven SOCs is not a one-time program: it's a continuous journey. As AI evolves, as threats change, and as the SOC's own processes mature, training needs to keep pace, ensuring that both technology and people evolve together. In the most successful SOCs, training isn't just about teaching analysts how to use AI: it's about showing them how to work with AI as a partner, each learning from the other in a constant cycle of improvement.

Measuring the Success of Human-Machine Collaboration

You can't improve what you don't measure. In SOCs, measuring human-machine collaboration is just as important as tracking detection speed or response times. Organizations invest in AI expecting faster threat detection and smarter analysis, but true success isn't just about speed. It's about how well AI and analysts work together to build a stronger, more resilient SOC.

One key metric is Mean Time to Detect (MTTD) and Mean Time to Respond (MTTR). AI should help surface critical threats faster and provide enriched context, reducing the time analysts spend on manual investigation. But while these numbers show efficiency, they don't measure trust or collaboration.

A more insightful metric is *Analyst Confidence in AI Recommendations*. Regular feedback loops where analysts rate AI-generated correlations, risk scores, and playbook recommendations reveal whether AI is truly assisting or just adding noise. Higher confidence and lower overrides over time indicate that analysts trust AI's reasoning and rely on its insights.

Kindo actively supports this process, capturing analyst feedback in real time. Every accepted, modified, or rejected AI recommendation is logged, not just to improve detection models but also to track trust-building over time. A steady rise in AI-assisted decisions shows that collaboration is maturing.

Another crucial factor is *Incident Quality at Escalation*. In a well-tuned SOC, senior analysts should only see meaningful, high-priority cases already enriched with context, artifacts, and next steps. If AI correctly filters noise and prioritizes risk, false escalations decrease, allowing experts to focus on true threats.

Success is reflected in *Analyst Retention and Satisfaction*. AI should eliminate grunt work, reduce alert fatigue, and turn investigations into a strategic process. When AI augments analysts rather than replacing them, burnout drops, and job satisfaction rises.

The real measure of success is in how fast AI works and how well it empowers analysts. A truly collaborative SOC automates, learns, adapts, and grows stronger with every decision human and AI make together.

Case Studies — Human and Machine Working Together

The theory of human-machine collaboration sounds promising, but the real test lies in practice. Across the Gulf region and beyond, forward-thinking organizations have already embraced AI-powered SOCs, blending automation with human expertise to achieve remarkable operational improvements. These case studies highlight how collaboration becomes a force multiplier when done right.

Case Study 1: Financial Sector SOC

A leading financial institution in the UAE faced a rising tide of phishing and credential-based attacks targeting both employees and customers. Traditionally, analysts manually correlated email logs, endpoint data, and identity access patterns to reconstruct phishing campaigns after they were already active.

After deploying AI-driven detection and correlation, supported by a platform like Kindo, this process changed dramatically. AI automatically correlated email headers, login attempts, and lateral movement signals across the network, surfacing not just isolated alerts but complete attack chains; mapped from initial phishing email to compromised endpoint to privilege escalation attempts. Analysts were no longer chasing fragments; they started with the whole story in front of them. With Kindo's ability to explain every step taken in its analysis, analysts quickly trusted the machine's reasoning, using that time saved to harden email filtering rules and enhance user awareness programs.

Case Study 2: Government Entity SOC

In a large government SOC managing critical infrastructure assets, analysts struggled with sheer data volume. Network telemetry, OT system logs, cloud application data, and endpoint signals generated hundreds of thousands of daily events: too many for human teams to handle manually.

The SOC introduced human-machine pairing workflows, where AI handled first-pass analysis, flagging anomalies based on historical baselines and contextual intelligence. Analysts reviewed only high-confidence, contextually enriched incidents, with AI explaining why the anomaly mattered in the context of critical assets and known attack patterns. This approach cut alert fatigue by more than half, while simultaneously increasing detection accuracy: a direct outcome of AI filtering noise without removing real threats. Analysts saw AI as a productivity partner, not a replacement.

Case Study 3: Retail Group SOC

A multi-national retail group operating across the GCC struggled to scale its SOC operations across multiple regions. Each regional team had its own processes, tools, and data sources, creating gaps in visibility and inconsistent threat detection.

The group adopted a centralized AI platform, where AI agents collected and correlated data from all regional SOCs into a single pane of glass. Analysts in each region could see localized incidents enriched with global context: learning from patterns observed in other regions. AI ensured that detection logic adapted locally while maintaining a consistent global threat view. This harmonized approach empowered regional analysts with better visibility while reducing operational fragmentation.

In all these cases, success was not driven by AI alone, it was the result of thoughtful orchestration between AI automation and human intelligence. Platforms like Kindo are making this possible by ensuring that automation was explainable, customizable, and aligned with each organization's specific operating model. Analysts retained their strategic role, while AI amplified their speed, coverage, and precision.

The takeaway is clear: human-machine collaboration is not a compromise between speed and trust. When built correctly, it delivers both, a SOC that operates at machine speed with human insight, turning every analyst into a smarter, faster decision-maker.

The Future Belongs to Human-Machine Teams

The most successful SOCs of tomorrow will not be fully automated, nor will they remain purely human-operated. The future belongs to hybrid SOCs, where AI amplifies human capability and humans sharpen AI performance: a collaborative intelligence loop that continuously strengthens itself.

This collaboration is a technical upgrade and a cultural shift. Analysts no longer see AI as a replacement, but as a teammate that handles the heavy lifting, clears the noise, and accelerates the path to understanding and action. Meanwhile, AI systems, such as Kindo, don't just automate in isolation, they learn from every human decision, evolving detection logic and playbooks in ways that reflect both real-world threats and organizational preferences.

The organizations that get this balance right will have a double advantage: operational efficiency and cultural resilience. Their SOCs will run faster, smarter, and with less burnout, while also retaining the flexibility and creativity that only human intelligence can bring.

This brings us naturally to the next crucial topic: how to actually implement AI in SOCs, step by step. Because technology alone won't drive transformation. Success lies in how AI is introduced, integrated, governed, and continuously improved. In the next chapter, we dive into the practical best practices for bringing AI into your SOC, not just as a tool, but as a trusted and essential part of your team.

Chapter Twelve

Implementing AI in SOCs: Best Practices

The SOC war room was buzzing. A major incident had just been contained in record time — what would have taken six hours a year ago had been triaged, analyzed, and escalated in under one. The difference? AI was now part of the team.

The SOC manager turned to his team. "A year ago, we would've been drowning in logs, trying to piece this together manually. Now, AI surfaces the right insights instantly, and we act faster."

This is what successful AI adoption looks like — not replacing analysts, but giving them the tools to work smarter, not harder. Yet, getting here wasn't just about installing new technology. It required rethinking how the SOC operated, trusting AI to handle repetitive tasks, and ensuring every AI-driven insight was actionable.

Setting Clear Objectives

AI should never be introduced just because it's trendy: it must solve real SOC pain points. Whether the goal is to reduce false positives, accelerate detection, enrich incident context, or automate reporting, defining clear objectives is the foundation for success. Without clear objectives, even the most powerful AI becomes just another underutilized tool in an overcrowded stack.

Kindo helps SOCs define this purpose upfront, aligning AI use cases with actual operational bottlenecks. Whether the SOC struggles with alert fatigue, inconsistent correlation, or fragmented playbooks, Kindo ensures AI is not just added, but applied to the problems that slow the SOC down.

Conducting a Realistic Gap Assessment

Once objectives are set, the next step is to assess where the SOC stands today in terms of:

- **Technology readiness** – Are current tools and platforms AI-compatible?
- **Data quality** – AI thrives on clean, structured, and well-governed data.

- **Process maturity** – Are workflows structured enough for automation?
- **Team readiness** – Do analysts trust and understand AI-driven workflows?

This assessment isn't about judging the team: it's about understanding the foundation AI will be built on. A rushed AI implementation without addressing these gaps will lead to frustration, distrust, and ultimately, failure.

The key to success? *AI should work for the SOC, not the other way around.*

Forming the AI Task Force – Cross-Functional Ownership

One of the most critical success factors in any AI implementation is shared ownership. AI in the SOC doesn't belong solely to the security team or the IT department: it sits at the intersection of technology, operations, governance, and compliance. This is why successful organizations start by forming a dedicated AI Task Force, bringing together: SOC leadership, Security analysts, IT teams, Compliance officers, Data science specialists (if available).

This task force is not a one-time committee, it acts as the governance anchor throughout the AI lifecycle. From initial deployment to tuning, auditing, and expanding AI use cases, the task force ensures AI evolves alongside the SOC's maturity and business needs.

Kindo fits naturally into this cross-functional model because it's not just a detection engine: it's a collaborative platform that touches threat intelligence ingestion, playbook automation, reporting, and compliance documentation. By working with the entire SOC ecosystem, Kindo ensures AI doesn't operate in isolation, it becomes part of the fabric of daily operations, with clear accountability at every stage.

This cross-functional ownership also helps manage *change resistance*, a common challenge when introducing automation into established workflows. When analysts see that their input shaped the AI's configuration, they are more likely to trust its outputs. When compliance sees that governance requirements were embedded from day one, audits become smoother. And when leadership sees that AI adoption aligns directly with business resilience goals, executive buy-in grows stronger.

The AI Task Force is the bridge between technology and trust. It ensures AI adoption is both operationally effective and culturally accepted, turning AI into a trusted ally rather than an imposed tool.

Enterprise-Ready Security: Ensuring AI Governance and Compliance

Adopting AI in security operations is all about

- Automation,
- Efficiency,
- Ensuring security,
- Compliance, and
- Governance at scale.

Modern enterprises require robust security frameworks to protect their digital assets and align with regulatory mandates and corporate risk policies.

Kindo is designed with enterprise security in mind, providing built-in mechanisms for governance, compliance, and data protection. Organizations leveraging AI for cybersecurity need clear controls over how AI operates within their infrastructure, ensuring that automation enhances security rather than introducing new risks.

Key Enterprise Security Features in Kindo

Kindo offers the following enterprise-grade security features to ensure responsible AI implementation:

- **Centralized Access Controls:** Fine-grained, role-based access control ensures only authorized personnel can interact with AI-driven workflows.

- **Data Loss Prevention Mechanisms:** AI-powered monitoring detects anomalies in data transfers, preventing leaks and unauthorized data exfiltration.

- **Audit Logging & Traceability:** Every AI action, decision, and intervention is logged for full visibility, ensuring compliance with security frameworks such as ISO 27001, GDPR, and NIST CSF.

- **Regulatory Compliance Alignment:** Kindo aligns with global and regional regulations (such as UAE NESA, SAMA, and NCA ECC) to ensure AI-driven SOCs remain fully compliant with legal mandates.

By embedding these enterprise-ready security controls, Kindo enables organizations to deploy AI-driven SOC solutions with confidence, ensuring security teams maintain full operational oversight while benefiting from automation.

Phased Rollout — Starting Small, Scaling Smart

The fastest way to fail with AI in a SOC is to launch everything at once, hoping the system will magically solve every problem overnight. AI is a learning technology, and like any learner, it performs best when it starts small, builds confidence, and gradually expands its responsibilities. This is why phased rollout is the recommended path for real-world AI adoption in SOCs.

The first phase is the observation phase: Focuses on understanding the data. AI is integrated into existing SOC tools, observing alert flows, analyst actions, and incident handling processes, but without taking autonomous action. During this phase, Kindo, for example, passively analyzes incident data, correlates patterns, and compares its own logic to human decisions, learning how the SOC thinks before suggesting its own responses.

Once the observation phase builds a baseline understanding, *the second phase is assisted automation* begins. AI starts offering recommendations, enriching incidents with context and proposed next steps, but leaving the final decision to analysts. This allows analysts to validate AI logic in real-time, building trust while also providing continuous feedback to fine-tune detection and response playbooks.

Only after AI has demonstrated consistent value and earned analyst trust does the *SOC enter autonomous mode,* where low-risk, repetitive incidents are handled end-to-end by the AI, freeing analysts to focus on high-risk, complex cases. Even in this autonomous phase, platforms like Kindo ensure every action remains fully transparent and auditable, preserving human oversight over the entire system.

This crawl-walk-run approach minimizes operational disruption, gives analysts time to adapt to their evolving roles, and ensures the AI is properly tuned to real-world data before taking direct action. It also helps identify unexpected gaps, like missing data sources or inconsistent processes, that need to be addressed before full automation can succeed.

Phased rollout is not a sign of caution: it's a sign of maturity. SOCs that adopt AI gradually, with constant human feedback and performance tuning, create systems that evolve naturally alongside their operational needs. They avoid the shock of sudden automation while ensuring AI adds value from day one.

Self-Management in Kindo

One of the most innovative shifts in AI adoption inside SOCs comes from self-managed models and deployments: solutions that not only perform detection, enrichment, and response, but are also provisioned, hosted, and tuned within the organization's own infrastructure.

In Kindo's architecture, this approach is embodied through Self-Managed Kindo: a deployment model that allows full control over the product, whether running in a public cloud, hybrid environment, or on-premises infrastructure.

This capability includes the use of Self-Managed Models— generative AI models that are configured and maintained internally. These models may be self-hosted, trained to meet specific organizational needs, or securely integrated using cloud services that support compliance and data sovereignty requirements. For example, Kindo can be configured to use Anthropic's language models through trusted cloud infrastructure designed for regulated environments.

At the time of writing this book, these models are used as *User LLMs* (language models that respond to analysts' questions and assist with tasks upon request). In the future, support will also be added for *Worker LLMs* (models that can perform tasks automatically in the background without waiting for user input), enabling more autonomous AI-driven operations across the SOC.

By enabling self-managed configurations, Kindo ensures organizations retain full sovereignty over their AI systems — governing data flow, access, model behavior, and security boundaries. This dramatically reduces dependency on external service providers and gives SOC teams the autonomy to define how AI adapts and scales within their environment.

Kindo embeds self-assessment and continuous tuning directly into the AI engine. As incidents are processed, the system evaluates:

- How often its recommendations align with analyst decisions
- Which playbooks result in rapid containment vs. unnecessary escalations
- Whether false positive suppression rules are effective or need adjustment

This real-time introspection allows Kindo to adapt continuously, eliminating the need for infrequent, manual tuning cycles. Instead, the platform evolves dynamically with the organization's threat landscape.

Self-management also extends to telemetry awareness. If critical data sources stop reporting due to integration issues or misconfigurations, Kindo proactively notifies SOC managers—reducing the risk of unnoticed blind spots in fast-changing environments.

Importantly, self-management does not eliminate human oversight. Analysts interact with live dashboards that show system confidence, learning effectiveness, and areas where human input is valuable. This collaborative feedback loop ensures that AI and human analysts continuously refine one another in real time.

Audit Logs and Data Preservation — Keeping Track of Every Move

In any modern SOC, what happened matters just as much as what was done about it. This is even more critical when AI systems play an active role in detection, analysis, and response. Every action AI takes, every recommendation, every correlation, every automated decision, must be fully documented and preserved. Without robust audit trails, the SOC loses its ability to explain or defend past decisions, especially during regulatory reviews, internal audits, or post-incident investigations.

With Kindo, auditability is part of the core design. Every piece of data processed, every detection triggered, every enrichment applied, and every response initiated by Kindo is logged in a structured, time-stamped audit trail. This ensures SOC leaders can:

- Reconstruct any incident from alert to closure.
- See exactly which data sources contributed to each decision.
- Review which recommendations were accepted, modified, or rejected by analysts.
- Track every human-AI interaction, ensuring decisions were collaborative, not opaque.

But data preservation goes deeper than just recording system activity. In AI-powered SOCs, even the prompts analysts enter to request context, intelligence reports, or guidance need to be preserved and audited. This helps in two critical ways:

- It captures the reasoning process—showing what the analyst wanted to know and how AI responded.
- It helps detect inappropriate or risky queries, ensuring analysts don't inadvertently ask AI to generate content that violates corporate policies or regulatory norms.

Kindo maintains a full log of prompts and responses, tied directly to each incident's lifecycle. This provides a clear window into analyst thought processes, which becomes invaluable during post-incident reviews when leadership or auditors want to understand why certain decisions were made.

This level of transparency and preservation ensures that AI in the SOC is also accountable and defensible. In a world where regulators demand proof, not promises, having complete, searchable, and immutable audit logs is the difference between operational excellence and regulatory exposure.

DLP, Secrets Management, and Sensitive Data Preservation

When AI becomes a core part of the SOC, data handling responsibilities multiply. The AI is not just processing raw logs; it's enriching incidents with context from threat intelligence feeds, internal communications, and sometimes even data extracted from files attached to alerts. This means AI is constantly touching sensitive information, from credentials to PII to classified internal processes. Without careful data preservation and protection controls, the very system meant to secure the business could inadvertently become a data leakage risk.

This is where Data Loss Prevention (DLP) and secrets management play a critical role in the AI-SOC integration process. Every AI-enhanced process, whether it's automated playbook execution, incident enrichment, or contextual advisory generation, must operate under strict data handling policies. This includes:

- Masking or redacting sensitive fields when data is shared across systems.
- Automatically detecting and flagging any attempt to expose secrets (like passwords or API keys) within prompts, incident notes, or automated reports.
- Encrypting all stored data, both in transit and at rest, with role-based controls over who can access specific parts of the dataset.

Kindo is designed to preserve sensitive information without compromising operational speed. Its built-in secrets management ensures that credentials and confidential data are automatically masked when included in logs, alerts, or analyst queries. If an analyst accidentally requests advisory that touches sensitive fields, Kindo applies contextual DLP rules, preventing the unauthorized disclosure of that data while preserving the operational usefulness of the advisory itself.

This ensures that AI can act intelligently without overexposing the data that powers its intelligence. Every response generated by Kindo: whether it's a suggested response action or a contextual advisory, goes through a data sensitivity check, ensuring the output respects both corporate DLP policies and regulatory requirements.

Preserving data integrity, confidentiality, and auditability in AI-driven SOCs isn't optional: it's the foundation that keeps automation safe and compliant. With Kindo's fusion of speed, transparency, and sensitive data preservation, SOC teams gain the confidence to let AI work faster, knowing the system itself is governed by strong guardrails designed to protect the very data that defines their mission.

Embedding AI into SOC Playbooks and Operational Processes

AI in a SOC should not be an isolated tool, it must be an active participant in daily operations, seamlessly integrating into playbooks and workflows. When AI is embedded into incident response, it automates routine tasks, accelerates decision-making, and ensures analysts focus on what matters most.

Traditional playbooks follow fixed steps, often struggling to adapt to evolving threats. AI-driven SOCs replace static workflows with adaptive playbooks that adjust in real time based on live data, past incidents, and threat intelligence. AI can pre-fill investigation details, correlate related events, and suggest next steps, significantly reducing manual effort.

With Kindo, this happens effortlessly. The moment an incident is detected, AI enriches the case with risk scores, historical context, and recommended actions, ensuring analysts start with actionable intelligence rather than raw data. AI does not replace expertise—it enhances it by surfacing insights that would take hours to compile manually.

Beyond playbooks, AI enhances SOC performance by providing real-time insights into alert handling, areas requiring human intervention, and workflow optimization. Instead of relying on retrospective reviews, teams can actively refine operations as incidents unfold. Each processed incident contributes to ongoing refinement, ensuring the SOC becomes more efficient, adaptive, and responsive over time.

When AI is fully embedded into operations, it stops being just another tool, it becomes the SOC's force multiplier, evolving with every threat it encounters.

Step-by-Step Integration Process — From Idea to Reality

Step 1: Define Clear Goals and Objectives

Every successful AI adoption starts with one question: What are we solving for? Adding AI just because competitors are doing it, or because a vendor promised "100% automation," is a recipe for disappointment. AI must address specific pain points that the SOC already feels every day:

- Alert overload,
- Slow incident resolution,
- Gaps in visibility, or
- Inconsistent correlation across data sources.

Defining these goals doesn't happen in a vacuum. It requires talking to every stakeholder who touches incident management; from frontline analysts drowning in alerts to compliance officers struggling to generate audit reports under time pressure. These conversations reveal where manual work causes the most friction, making it clear where AI can add immediate value.

For example, in many SOCs, Tier 1 analysts spend 60-70% of their time enriching alerts; pulling logs from different tools, correlating user behavior, cross-checking with threat intelligence, and writing up initial incident reports. This is exactly the kind of repetitive, time-intensive work AI can automate. Allowing Tier 1 analysts to focus more on decision-making and less on data gathering.

With Kindo, this process becomes data driven. During pre-implementation workshops, Kindo helps SOCs map out their entire incident lifecycle, identifying the exact points where automation can save the most time. This isn't about theoretical AI capabilities; it's about tailoring AI use cases to the actual bottlenecks your team faces every day.

The result is a clear *AI charter*: a document that outlines:

- Which processes will be automated.
- What success looks like for each process.
- What data sources will feed the AI.
- Which human oversight points remain essential.
- How success will be measured.

This upfront clarity ensures AI deployment has purpose and focus and avoids the common pitfall of AI being underused after deployment because the team never really knew what they wanted it to do.

Step 2: Conduct a Comprehensive Gap Assessment

With goals defined, the next step is to assess your starting point. Before AI can enhance your SOC, you need a clear, honest understanding of your current processes, tools, data flows, and team capabilities. This gap assessment acts as a reality check, highlighting what's ready for automation and what needs fixing first.

The assessment should cover:

- **Process Maturity:** Are your workflows clearly documented? Are playbooks followed consistently, or do analysts improvise?
- **Tool Integration:** Do your SIEM, EDR, SOAR, and ticketing systems work together smoothly, or are they isolated silos?
- **Data Quality:** Is your log data normalized and enriched before analysis? Or are analysts working with incomplete, inconsistent data?

- **Skills and Training:** How comfortable are your analysts with AI-assisted workflows? Will they need training in interpreting AI output and providing structured feedback to improve AI performance?

- **Compliance Readiness:** Can you demonstrate, today, exactly how each incident was handled, and which data sources were involved? Is your current incident documentation process audit-ready?

This step isn't about judging the team; it's about understanding the environment AI is being introduced into. An AI platform, no matter how advanced, can't fix missing data sources, broken workflows, or lack of process ownership. That's why smart SOCs fix the foundations before layering AI on top.

Kindo ensures a smooth AI adoption process by aligning its deployment with the SOC's existing workflows, data sources, and operational needs. Instead of forcing rigid implementations, Kindo adapts to the organization's security ecosystem, ensuring AI is fed high-quality data and seamlessly integrates into established processes. This approach builds analyst confidence, making AI a trusted partner in daily operations rather than an external add-on.

Together, these first two steps (defining goals and understanding gaps) form the bedrock for successful AI deployment. Skip these, and even the best AI will become just another unused tool gathering dust. But get them right, and you set the stage for AI to become a transformative force inside your SOC.

Step 3: Create a Cross-Functional AI Task Force

AI in a SOC is a:

- Technology initiative,
- Cultural shift,
- Process overhaul, and
- Governance evolution all rolled into one.

This means no single team can own it entirely. Security analysts may understand the operational pain points, but they rely on IT to manage infrastructure, compliance to oversee governance, and leadership to align AI use cases with business goals. That's why successful SOCs create a dedicated *AI Task Force* before the first model is ever deployed.

The AI Task Force brings together representatives from:

- **SOC Operations:** To define use cases, pain points, and operational needs.
- **IT and Data Teams:** To ensure data pipelines, integrations, and log flows support AI's learning.
- **GRC and Legal:** To enforce data privacy, auditability, and regulatory alignment from day one.
- **Security Leadership:** To connect AI investment to business resilience and demonstrate ROI.
- **Data Science Specialists:** Guides model tuning, data strategy, and AI-driven optimization techniques.
- **Training and Development:** To map out upskilling needs and ensure all stakeholders understand AI's role.

This task force doesn't just guide the initial deployment, they own AI performance reviews, retraining schedules, and feedback loops throughout its lifecycle. They ensure AI evolves alongside the SOC, never drifting away from operational realities.

Kindo actively supports the Task Force process by offering structured implementation workshops where every stakeholder group works together to map:

- What processes will be AI-assisted.
- What human-AI handoffs are required.
- What data governance rules apply.
- What metrics define success.

This collaborative kickoff reduces resistance, builds cross-functional trust, and ensures AI adoption isn't seen as a top-down directive, but rather a shared initiative everyone has shaped, which we discussed earlier in this chapter also.

Step 4: Build Targeted Training for Every Role

Introducing AI into the SOC without proper training creates two predictable failures:

- Analysts either distrust the AI or override its recommendations, treating it as noise.

- Or they over-trust the AI, blindly following its outputs even when context calls for human intervention.

To avoid both extremes, training must start before deployment and continue as AI learns and evolves. This training isn't one-size-fits-all — each SOC role needs a tailored learning path:

- **Analysts:** Focus on interpreting AI-generated risk scores, investigating enriched incidents, and providing structured feedback to fine-tune models.

- **Team Leads:** Learn to monitor AI performance against KPIs, spot trends in AI-human collaboration, and guide playbook adjustments based on what AI is learning.

- **Compliance and Governance:** Focus on AI auditability — ensuring all actions taken (both by AI and analysts responding to AI) are documented in ways that satisfy regulators and internal policies.

- **Leadership:** Learn how to connect AI operational metrics (like MTTD and false positive rates) to business outcomes, turning AI's technical success into board-level narratives.

Kindo simplifies this training journey by providing explainability-by-design. Every detection, correlation, and response recommendation come with a "why" — clear, step-by-step logic showing how Kindo reached its conclusion. This helps analysts learn by doing, reinforcing AI literacy with every incident handled.

Training is not a one-time event. As AI evolves; adapting to new threats, new data sources, and analyst feedback, training must evolve too. Successful SOCs make AI training part of continuous development programs, ensuring analysts always understand how their digital teammate thinks.

Together, these steps (cross-functional ownership and targeted training) build the cultural foundation for AI success. SOC teams stop seeing AI as an external imposition and start seeing it as a trusted colleague they've personally helped shape.

Step 5: Identify and Deliver Quick Wins

The fastest way to build trust in AI isn't through long strategy documents or endless workshops, it's by delivering tangible value that analysts can see, feel, and benefit from immediately. This is where quick wins become essential to any AI rollout.

Quick wins are small, high-impact automations that immediately reduce analyst pain points without disrupting major processes. The best quick wins in SOCs tend to involve repetitive, time-consuming tasks that AI can handle reliably and consistently, for example:

- **Automating enrichment:** Instead of analysts manually gathering log data, threat intel, and asset context after every alert, AI pre-enriches every incident the moment it's detected.
- **Pre-filling incident reports:** AI captures all relevant metadata—timestamps, affected assets, alert sources—and drafts the initial report, allowing analysts to focus on the investigation rather than administration.

- **Noise filtering:** AI learns to recognize harmless patterns that generate frequent alerts, allowing these low-risk signals to be auto-closed unless a new risk factor emerges.

The beauty of quick wins is that they create positive momentum. Analysts see time saved immediately, SOC leaders see faster response times, and everyone starts trusting the AI to handle more over time. This creates a virtuous cycle where confidence builds through visible, practical results.

With Kindo, many of these quick wins are already pre-baked into the platform. Its autonomous enrichment, risk scoring, and report generation capabilities are designed to deliver instant value without requiring analysts to redesign their entire workflow on day one. This plug-and-play approach ensures Kindo starts earning trust from the very first incident it touches.

Step 6: Selecting the Right Tool, Solution, and Framework

AI is an ecosystem of capabilities, ranging from machine learning-powered detection to NLP-based advisory tools to automation engines that execute response actions. The trick is choosing tools that fit your SOC's maturity, goals, and data landscape, rather than chasing flashy marketing promises.

Key considerations when choosing an AI solution include:

- **Data Compatibility:** Can the AI ingest data from your current SIEM, EDR, and log sources without complex transformations?
- **Explainability:** Does the AI provide clear reasoning for its recommendations, so analysts can trust (and challenge) its outputs?
- **Integration Readiness:** Does the platform integrate natively with your existing workflows, including ITSM and SOAR tools?
- **Compliance Support:** Can the AI log its own decisions, maintaining a full audit trail to satisfy regulators and internal reviews?
- **Adaptability:** Can the AI evolve as your SOC matures — starting with enrichment, moving to detection, and ultimately handling automated response?

Kindo is designed with these criteria in mind. It's not a generic automation platform: it's built specifically for SOC

319

workflows, pre-integrated with common tools like SIEMs, EDRs, ticket systems, file storage systems, and threat intelligence platforms, always ready to adapt to your processes instead of forcing you to change for it. Combined with its built-in explainability, WhiteRabbitNeo, and audit features, Kindo delivers not only operational speed but also regulatory confidence: making it the right kind of AI for regulated SOC environments.

Choosing the right AI platform isn't about features: it's about finding the right partner for the long-term evolution of your SOC. One that fits your culture, understands your data, and grows alongside your needs.

Step 7: Run Simulations and Controlled Tests

No matter how powerful the AI platform is, you cannot afford to go live blindly. Before fully embedding AI into production workflows, the SOC needs to simulate real-world incidents in a controlled test environment, allowing both analysts and the AI itself to practice working together.

Simulations allow the SOC to:

- Test how AI correlates artifacts from multiple data sources.
- Evaluate how well AI-generated recommendations align with analyst expectations.
- Measure how AI performs under pressure: for example, handling multiple simultaneous incidents.
- Spot gaps in data feeds, enrichment quality, and playbook logic.

These exercises also build analyst confidence, giving them time to see the AI in action, ask questions, and validate its logic before real incidents depend on it.

This simulation phase is about more than testing the AI; it's about testing the collaboration between analysts and AI. This human-AI relationship is what defines whether automation becomes a trusted teammate or an ignored background tool.

Step 8: Develop Standard Operating Procedures (SOPs) for AI Workflows

AI changes how incidents are handled and that change needs to be codified into formal SOPs, ensuring every analyst, team lead, and auditor knows exactly how AI fits into the process.

SOPs should define:

- Which types of alerts are fully automated, and which always require human review.
- How analysts review AI recommendations, what questions to ask, what data to validate.
- How to escalate when AI logic seems flawed, ensuring there's a clear feedback path for improving detection rules.
- Who owns AI performance reviews, and how often models are retrained.

Clear SOPs improve efficiency and build trust. When everyone understands how and why AI is involved, they're far more likely to use it effectively.

Kindo supports this by embedding workflow transparency directly into its interface. Analysts see exactly which SOP triggered after an alert was detected, which enrichment steps were performed, and what historical patterns contributed to risk scoring. This procedural transparency reinforces SOP adherence without adding paperwork.

Step 9: Integrate AI with Legacy Systems

Most SOCs don't start with a clean slate. They already have legacy tools, custom scripts, and historical processes deeply embedded in their workflows. AI cannot replace all of this overnight. Successful adoption requires seamless integration, allowing AI to enhance, not disrupt, existing processes.

This means ensuring:

- AI can ingest data directly from legacy log collectors.
- Enriched alerts flow back into existing ticketing or case management tools.
- Analysts can pivot seamlessly from AI-enriched incidents back to original log sources if deeper investigation is needed.

Kindo was designed with this integration-first mindset. As of today, Kindo supports integrations with ticket systems, file storage systems, security tools, and anything that has data accessible via an API. This extensive integration capability allows organizations to connect Kindo's AI functionalities with a wide array of tools ensuring that however they have built their SOC toolkit you can enhancing workflow automation and operational efficiency by using Kindo as an AI powered single pane of glass which reads from existing systems, writes back into existing platforms, and works within your existing playbooks. This approach allows AI to enhance what's already working, rather than forcing the SOC to rebuild from scratch.

This integration step is often where AI projects stall or fail, because the SOC underestimated how hard legacy compatibility can be. Smart SOCs treat integration not as a technical afterthought, but as a critical success factor planned from day one.

Step 10: Testing, Quality Assessment, and Performance Reviews

Once AI is integrated and playbooks are updated, the job isn't over, it's just getting started. AI in SOCs isn't like traditional software that you deploy and forget. It needs continuous testing, tuning, and quality reviews to ensure it evolves with the threat landscape and operational realities.

Testing doesn't stop at initial simulations. SOCs should conduct:

- Regular tabletop exercises to test AI-enhanced workflows under pressure.
- Periodic replay of real historical incidents, allowing the team to compare how AI would have handled them now versus how they were handled originally.
- Spot checks, where team leads audit AI-enriched cases, ensuring data accuracy, enrichment relevance, and recommendation quality meet evolving SOC standards.

These quality assessments ensure that AI doesn't drift away from reality, and analysts can see how their feedback has shaped the system over time.

With Kindo, these reviews become part of the operational DNA. Every incident handled by Kindo can automatically feed a performance review dashboard, showing:

- Which recommendations were accepted, modified, or rejected.
- Average time saved per incident.
- Enrichment success rates (did Kindo pull all relevant logs and intelligence correctly?).
- False positive and false negative rates over time.

This embedded review process ensures AI isn't just a tool in the corner, it's part of the continuous improvement cycle of the SOC itself.

Step 11: Build Continuous Feedback Loops

AI learns best from the analysts who work with it every day. Every time an analyst overrides a recommendation, adjusts a risk score, or provides additional context, that decision should flow directly into AI retraining pipelines, making the system smarter for the next case.

Feedback loops need to be:

- **Easy for analysts to provide.** No extra paperwork: just a simple "accept," "modify," or "reject" directly within the SOC platform.

- **Visible to the team.** Analysts need to see how their feedback influences future cases, reinforcing the message that they are shaping the AI.
- **Part of daily rhythm.** Reviewing AI performance and analyst feedback should become a standing agenda item in weekly SOC reviews.

Kindo builds this loop into its core design. Analysts don't just use Kindo; their interactions contribute to a growing knowledge base that refines its performance. Feedback is captured as data, enhancing future enrichment, correlation, and playbook execution. It enables fine-tuning by leveraging past interactions, ensuring that it isn't just automating tasks but optimizing itself to align with how the SOC thinks and operates.

Step 12: Monitor and Evaluate AI Performance Continuously

AI performance metrics should never be an afterthought, they should be part of the SOC's daily visibility, sitting alongside

327

traditional operational metrics like MTTD and MTTR. Key performance indicators for AI include:

- Accuracy of detection and correlation. How often is AI right?
- False positive suppression success. Is noise going down?
- Time saved per incident. Are analysts spending less time on basic tasks?
- Analyst confidence in AI recommendations. Are they trusting or bypassing AI insights?
- Compliance audit readiness. Can AI-driven processes stand up to regulatory scrutiny?

Kindo's performance monitoring capabilities provide data for these kinds of insights out of the box, allowing SOC leaders to see AI effectiveness evolve. This visibility ensures AI isn't just doing work, it is delivering measurable, provable value aligned with the SOC's broader performance goals.

The ultimate goal of this entire 12-step process is simple: AI should become a trusted, embedded partner, constantly learning and improving alongside the humans it supports. It should never become a black box or an unaccountable automation layer. When implemented using this measured, transparent approach, AI enhances both operational efficiency and organizational resilience, positioning the SOC not just to handle today's threats, but to continuously adapt to tomorrow's unknowns.

Challenges and Mitigation Strategies for Implementing AI in SOCs

While AI brings undeniable value to modern SOCs, successful adoption is rarely straightforward. Many organizations encounter unexpected hurdles, ranging from technical friction to cultural resistance. A mature SOC doesn't avoid challenges: it anticipates them, plans for them, and builds mitigation strategies into the AI adoption roadmap.

High Initial Investment and Operational Costs

Deploying AI in a SOC isn't just a technology expense but involves training, process redesign, data pipeline readiness, and governance setup. Many organizations underestimate these hidden costs, assuming AI is a plug-and-play solution. This mindset leads to frustration and budget overruns.

Mitigation: The AI Task Force should map every cost element upfront, from licensing to integration to training, and secure budget commitment for the full lifecycle, not just for the first year. With solutions like Kindo, costs become more predictable because integration templates, pre-configured playbooks, and training modules are part of the offering, reducing expensive custom development.

Talent Shortage and Skill Gaps

AI in SOCs requires a new blend of skills, analysts who not only investigate threats but also understand how to interpret AI-driven correlations, provide structured feedback, and influence model retraining. Most traditional SOC teams aren't equipped for this shift from manual responder to collaborative trainer.

Mitigation: This is where role-specific AI training becomes essential, with separate learning paths for analysts, leads, compliance teams, and IT operators. With Kindo, every user sees a tailored interface and explanation depth aligned to their role, ensuring the technology feels intuitive, not intimidating.

Integration with Legacy Systems

AI's effectiveness depends heavily on data quality and completeness. Legacy SOC tools often lack modern APIs, produce inconsistent log formats, or rely on manual data transfers that break the real-time flow AI needs.

Mitigation: AI deployment should always start with a data readiness review, ensuring every log source is complete, normalized, and accessible. Tools like Kindo come with pre-built connectors for common SIEM, EDR, and threat intelligence platforms, reducing custom integration work and ensuring AI starts with clean, reliable data.

Resistance to Change

One of the biggest blockers to successful AI adoption is cultural resistance from analysts who fear that automation will replace their jobs or devalue their expertise. This fear, if unaddressed, can sabotage adoption from within: analysts ignore AI recommendations, double-check every automated action, or quietly bypass the tool altogether.

Mitigation: Building trust in AI starts long before deployment. Analysts need to be part of the design process, helping shape playbooks, tuning enrichment logic, and training the system using real incidents. When analysts see their fingerprints on the AI's logic, they are far more likely to trust its outputs.

Kindo supports this by making the feedback loop highly visible, every analyst decision trains the system, and analysts can see how their input improves future detections. This reinforces the idea that AI is a partner, not a replacement.

Ensuring Data Quality and Reducing Dirty Data Risks

AI models are only as good as the data they ingest. Inconsistent timestamps, missing logs, duplicate events, or incomplete enrichment data can corrupt model training, leading to missed detections or unreliable recommendations.

Mitigation: AI platforms should include data health monitoring, alerting SOC managers when critical feeds drop, data anomalies appear, or enrichment sources fall out of sync. Kindo includes real-time data pipeline monitoring, helping SOC teams spot data quality issues before they impact AI performance.

Bias, Fairness, and Explainability

AI trained on historically biased data can inherit those biases, unfairly flagging certain behaviors or users as higher risk — even when those behaviors are innocent in context. SOCs that blindly trust AI, without reviewing how decisions were made, expose themselves to ethical and legal risks.

Mitigation: Explainability is mandatory. Every AI recommendation must include the data sources, logic steps, and historical references that influenced the decision. With Kindo, explainability is built into every detection, ensuring analysts never see a black box, only a clear, auditable reasoning trail.

These challenges are real, but they are not showstoppers. With proactive planning, structured governance, and the right technology partner, SOCs can turn each challenge into a learning opportunity, gradually building a resilient, AI-enhanced operational model.

Measuring and Evaluating AI Impact — Linking Technology to Business Outcomes

Every technology investment in the SOC, especially AI, must answer one core question: What value does it create, operationally and for the business? It's easy to get caught up in technical performance metrics, but ultimately, AI's success should be measured by how well it reduces risk, improves efficiency, and enhances resilience.

To measure AI's real impact, SOCs need a layered set of KPIs, each connecting operational performance back to business objectives. These include:

Operational KPIs

- **Mean Time to Detect (MTTD):** How much faster are threats detected with AI-enhanced correlation and enrichment?
- **Mean Time to Respond (MTTR):** How much faster does the SOC resolve incidents when AI pre-enriches cases and triggers adaptive playbooks?
- **False Positive Reduction:** What percentage of previously escalated alerts are now

automatically filtered by AI without analyst intervention?

- **Incident Documentation Time:** How much time is saved in compiling incident reports when AI pre-fills reports with enriched context and artifacts?

Human Factors KPIs

- **Analyst Efficiency:** How many incidents can each analyst handle per shift compared to the pre-AI baseline?
- **AI Recommendation Acceptance Rate:** How often do analysts accept AI's suggested actions or categorizations, indicating growing trust in the system?
- **Reduction in Manual Enrichment:** What percentage of incident enrichment tasks are now automated?

Compliance and Governance KPIs

- **Audit Readiness:** How often can the SOC generate complete, audit-ready incident timelines and reports on demand, using AI-generated documentation?

- **Explainability Confidence:** How consistently can AI decisions be explained to auditors, leadership, or regulators without requiring reverse-engineering?

Business Outcome KPIs

- **Reduction in Downtime:** When AI reduces detection and response times, how does this translate into reduced business disruption?

- **Cost Avoidance:** By improving efficiency and reducing manual effort, how much operational cost is saved per incident?

- **Regulatory Performance:** How often does AI-enhanced documentation help the SOC pass audits or regulatory reviews smoothly?

Kindo's Role in Measuring Impact

One of the most common challenges SOCs face after deploying AI is tracking these metrics effectively. Most traditional platforms don't automatically capture AI performance data leaving SOC leaders to rely on manual reporting or fragmented dashboards.

Kindo addresses this directly by providing a dedicated AI Performance Dashboard, which tracks:

- How many incidents AI enriched, correlated, or resolved autonomously.
- Average time saved per incident due to automation.
- Analyst feedback loops — tracking how often analysts agree or override AI suggestions.
- A Trust Index, showing how AI confidence evolves over time.

This built-in visibility allows SOC leaders to quantify AI's contribution in clear, measurable terms: connecting faster detection and resolution directly to reduced risk, lower operational costs, and improved regulatory standing.

The goal isn't to create a data overload — it's to ensure every SOC leader can walk into a boardroom or regulatory review and confidently say:

"Here's how AI helps us respond faster, reduce risk, and keep the business running smoothly."

Measuring and Evaluating AI Impact — Linking Technology to Business Outcomes

Bringing AI into a SOC is about adding new capabilities, delivering measurable improvements across operations, security posture, and business resilience. If the SOC cannot clearly show how AI has improved performance, leadership may quickly question the value of the investment. That's why measuring and evaluating AI impact is just as important as the initial deployment itself.

AI effectiveness should be measured across three dimensions:

1. **Operational Efficiency**

This is the most immediate and visible area of impact. Key metrics include: MTTD, MTTR, Analyst Productivity which we already discussed earlier.

With Kindo, these operational KPIs can be collected via AI analysis and reported on, giving SOC managers visibility into how much time Kindo is saving and where those efficiency gains are occurring.

2. Detection and Accuracy

Speed means nothing if AI misfires, drowning analysts in false positives or, worse, missing real threats. Evaluating detection quality requires:

- **False Positive Rate (FPR)** — How often does AI escalate harmless events?
- **False Negative Rate (FNR)** — How often does AI miss actual threats?
- **Incident Quality at Escalation** — Are AI-enriched incidents well-prepared, with all necessary context provided upfront?

Kindo tracks these quality metrics over time, showing how AI's precision improves with feedback, ensuring that automation becomes smarter with every incident handled.

3. Strategic Impact

Beyond operational KPIs, AI should also contribute to broader business resilience. This means:

- Fewer security incidents escalating into full-blown crises.
- Faster reporting for regulatory compliance.

- Improved analyst satisfaction, reducing burnout and turnover.
- Enhanced board-level reporting, with clear linkage between SOC performance and risk reduction.

This is where AI-enhanced reporting (automatically correlating operational metrics to business impact) helps bridge the gap between technical teams and executive leadership. With Kindo, these reports can be automatically generated, connecting incident data directly to risk reduction narratives that leadership can understand.

Continuous Evaluation and Refinement

Measuring AI's impact is an ongoing process. Performance reviews should be embedded into SOC governance cycles, ensuring:

- AI models are regularly retrained on the latest threats and analyst feedback.
- Detection logic evolves with new tactics, techniques, and procedures (TTPs).
- Analysts continue to trust AI recommendations as transparency and accuracy improve.

This continuous evaluation ensures that AI doesn't stagnate, and that the SOC continues to capture value long after the initial deployment glow fades. In the most successful SOCs, measuring AI impact becomes part of the SOC's core performance management, ensuring automation aligns not just with operational efficiency, but with the organization's broader security and business goals.

Sustaining AI Success — From Implementation to Continuous Evolution

With AI now embedded into SOC workflows, the true journey begins ensuring its long-term relevance, accuracy, and value. AI is not a static technology; its strength lies in its ability to learn, adapt, and improve continuously. However, this requires the SOC team to actively nurture this evolution, treating AI not as a finished product but as a living system that evolves alongside the organization's security posture and the ever-changing threat landscape.

Cultivating the Feedback Culture

SOCs that thrive with AI don't just use it but collaborate with it. Every time an analyst overrides a recommendation, manually enriches an incident, or flags a false positive, that interaction helps refine security operations. Successful AI adoption depends on embedding feedback loops into daily workflows, ensuring the system adapts based on real-world experience.

Kindo is designed to seamlessly integrate feedback into its operations. Every analyst decision—whether escalating, adjusting severity, or modifying response actions—not only resolves an incident but also collects the data needed to enhance future detection logic. Analysts don't need to fill out extra forms or process reviews; their natural interactions with the platform create a structured feedback mechanism. This ensures that Kindo evolves in sync with the SOC's unique environment, making AI a collaborative partner rather than an isolated system.

Beyond Automation—AI as an Advisor

While early AI adoption often focuses on automating repetitive tasks; enrichment, noise filtering, and correlation, the real power of AI emerges when it acts as an advisor. Kindo learns the organization's infrastructure nuances, risk appetite, and historical incident patterns; it shifts from being reactive tools to a proactive risk advisor.

In this advisory role, Kindo doesn't just highlight suspicious activities, it begins to suggest how to optimize detection logic, improve data sources, and even adjust playbooks based on patterns the analysts themselves might not notice. This advisory intelligence empowers SOC leaders to transition from operational firefighting to strategic risk management, elevating the SOC's role within the broader security program.

The Power of Transparent Metrics

Successful SOCs understand that visibility drives both operational excellence and leadership support. That's why Kindo embedded transparent performance dashboards directly into their workflows, automatically tracking:

- *Time saved* through enrichment automation.
- *False positive reduction* achieved through refined detection tuning.
- *Analyst feedback trends,* showing where human trust in AI recommendations is rising and where it still needs work.

This performance visibility ensures SOC leaders always have real-time evidence of how AI enhances operational performance, links to business resilience, and delivers tangible value.

From Technology to Trusted Partnership

Ultimately, the success of AI in the SOC is not measured by its technical sophistication alone but by how seamlessly it becomes part of the team's mindset, culture, and daily rhythm. In SOCs that successfully adopt Kindo, analysts see AI not as a threat to their jobs, but as a trusted partner, one that lightens their workload, sharpens their decision-making, and helps them focus on the threats that truly matter.

This transformation (from tool to teammate) marks the true destination for AI adoption in SOCs. With this partnership firmly in place, the stage is set for the next and final discussion: turning today's AI implementation into tomorrow's continuous advantage.

Turning Best Practices into Daily Habits

The successful adoption of AI in a SOC hinges on technology, rests firmly on operational discipline, cultural alignment, and an ongoing commitment to learning and adaptation. AI in modern SOCs is not a one-time deployment or a static tool;

it's a living, evolving capability that grows smarter every day, fueled by real-world incidents, analyst feedback, and shifting threat landscapes.

Best practices only have value when they become part of the SOC's muscle memory, not as rigid steps in a project plan, but as flexible habits that guide how the team works. Forming an empowered AI Task Force that owns both governance and performance, embedding AI insights directly into playbooks and decision workflows, and fostering a feedback culture where every analyst interaction enhances future detection: these aren't optional extras. They're the core ingredients that turn AI into a trusted operational asset. With AI first tools now in market like Kindo it is now possible to bring in a collaborative engine that works side-by-side with analysts, enriching incidents with context, evolving its recommendations based on human feedback, and providing full transparency into every decision it makes. This transparency helps build the essential trust bridge between analysts and automation, ensuring that AI doesn't operate in a silo, but thrives as part of a human-AI partnership.

Ultimately, the most important measure of AI success is the level of trust and ownership the SOC team feels toward the system. When analysts see their expertise reflected in the AI's decisions, and leadership sees measurable improvements in both operational efficiency and risk reduction, AI shifts from being "just another tool" to becoming an indispensable teammate.

This mindset shift—*from automation tool to operational partner*—is what distinguishes truly resilient SOCs.

Conclusion — From Innovation to Resilience: The SOC's New Era

As we reach the final pages of this journey, one truth stands clear, the integration of AI into Security Operations Centers has transitioned from a novel innovation to an operational necessity. In an era where cyber threats are increasingly sophisticated, traditional manual processes are insufficient. AI enhances threat detection, automates incident response, and provides comprehensive visibility into security ecosystems, enabling organizations to stay ahead of adversaries.

However, the adoption of AI in cybersecurity is not without challenges. Organizations face technical hurdles in data integration, concerns about reliability, and ethical considerations regarding AI algorithms and data collection biases. Additionally, regulatory and compliance issues arise as AI advancements often outpace existing legal frameworks.

New AI first tools like Kindo address these challenges by offering a platform that securely adopts and centrally manages AI across the entire workforce. AI first Kindo empowers workforce productivity while maintaining security, compliance, and centralized management for IT and security teams.

The AI-driven transformation of SOCs is imperative for organizations aiming to enhance their cybersecurity posture. By embracing new powerful AI technologies organizations can navigate the complexities of modern cyber threats, ensuring resilience and operational excellence in their security operations.

What We've Learned Along the Way

Throughout this book, we explored how AI touches every facet of modern SOC operations. From detecting threats faster, to automating response, enriching context, predicting future attacks, and even shaping analyst workflows through human-machine collaboration. AI is no longer just about faster alerts; it's about smarter, context-aware decision-making. It's about reducing noise without losing sight of subtle, evolving threats. Most importantly, it's about enabling human analysts to operate at their full potential, free from repetitive drudgery, focused on creative investigation, proactive hunting, and strategic improvement.

We uncovered not only the opportunities AI presents, but also the challenges, from ethical governance and bias mitigation, to ensuring transparency and maintaining analyst trust. AI in the SOC must walk a delicate balance: fast enough to keep pace with machine-speed threats, but accountable enough to withstand regulatory scrutiny and maintain operational transparency.

The Role of Kindo — A Living Example of What's Possible

At many points in this book, Kindo emerged not as a product placement, but as a first to market working AI first example of how real-world SOCs can embrace AI responsibly and effectively. By embedding automation, enrichment, and leveraging historical interaction data for refinement, Kindo doesn't just make SOCs faster. It makes them smarter, more predictable, and increasingly self-improving with every incident handled. Its need of the hour, SOC needs transformation 'now now.'

Kindo's approach to self-management enables AI to assess its own accuracy, incorporate relevant data sources, and refine responses based on evolving threats. While AI models do not yet continually learn on their own, Kindo maintains a comprehensive log of user and AI interactions, allowing for fine-tuning that enhances performance over time. This offers a glimpse of what the SOC of the future will look like: an environment where automation is intelligent, adaptable, and always aligned with the organization's risk appetite and operational reality.

A Call to Action — Future-Proofing the SOC Starts Today

The message is clear standing still is no longer an option. SOC leaders can no longer afford to view AI as an experimental add-on, or worse, as a future project. *AI is here.* Attackers are using it. Regulators are expecting it. And SOC teams are depending on it to break free from the alert fatigue and process bottlenecks that have crippled their ability to stay ahead.

The path forward is not about replacing human analysts with machines, nor is it about chasing technology for technology's sake. It's about building smarter processes, clearer governance, and healthier collaboration between human expertise and machine intelligence. It's about treating AI not as a tool, but as a partner, one that learns alongside the SOC, shares its memory across shifts, and amplifies the skills of every analyst, from the most junior to the most senior.

As you close this book and return to your own SOC, I encourage you to ask yourself

- Where is your team spending its time today?
- Is it adding value through creative thinking, threat modeling, and proactive defense?
- Or is it stuck firefighting, chasing alerts, and manually stitching logs into incident reports?

Your answer to that question will tell you exactly where your AI journey needs to begin.

The Next Chapter Belongs to You

AI will not replace the SOC. But the SOCs that fail to embrace AI will be replaced by those that do. This book has given you the roadmap, the principles, some tool ideas, and the best practices. Now, it's up to you to write the next chapter in your organization's security story.

The future belongs to the augmented SOC—one where humans and machines work side by side, learning from each other, adapting faster than attackers can innovate, and turning every incident into a source of strength. This is not just the future of SOCs — it is the future of resilient business itself.

Glossary

Access Control: A security technique that regulates who or what can view or use resources in a computing environment, ensuring that only authorized users have access to specific data or systems.

Advanced Persistent Threat (APT): A long-term targeted cyberattack in which an intruder gains access to a network and remains undetected for an extended period to steal sensitive data.

Advanced Threat Detection: Techniques and tools used to identify sophisticated cyber threats that often evade traditional security measures.

Adversarial AI: Refers to techniques used by attackers to manipulate AI models, often by injecting misleading data to evade detection or cause incorrect predictions.

Artificial Intelligence (AI): The simulation of human intelligence by machines, enabling them to perform tasks such as decision-making, problem-solving, and learning from data.

Artificial Intelligence for IT Operations (AIOps): The use of AI and machine learning to automate IT operations, enhance performance monitoring, and predict issues before they impact business functions.

AI-Driven SOC: A Security Operations Center that leverages AI technologies to enhance threat detection, incident response, and overall cybersecurity operations.

AI First: A design principle that considers the use of AI from first principles in order to maximize the effectiveness of AI's impact versus the various attempts by legacy software vendors to bolt-on AI to outdated thinking and frameworks.

AI Governance: The framework and processes that ensure the ethical, transparent, and effective use of AI technologies within an organization.

Algorithm Bias: The systematic and unfair influence that can occur in AI algorithms, often resulting in discriminatory outcomes based on race, gender, or other factors.

Algorithm: A set of rules or instructions given to a computer to help it solve problems or perform tasks.

Attack Vectors: The methods or pathways used by cybercriminals to gain unauthorized access to a network or system.

Automation in SOC: The use of automated tools and technologies to streamline security operations, reduce manual workload, and enhance efficiency within a SOC.

Behavioral Analysis: A cybersecurity technique that identifies abnormal user or system behavior that could indicate a security threat.

Blue Team: A cybersecurity team responsible for defending an organization's networks, systems, and data from attacks by continuously monitoring and improving security posture.

Business Email Compromise (BEC): A type of cybercrime where an attacker gains access to a business email account and uses it to conduct fraudulent activities.

Business Process Automation (BPA): The use of technology to automate complex business processes and workflows, improving efficiency and reducing human intervention.

California Consumer Privacy Act (CCPA): A state law that enhances privacy rights and consumer protection for residents of California by regulating how businesses collect, use, and share personal data.

Computer Vision: A field of artificial intelligence that enables machines to interpret and understand visual data from the world, often used in security applications like facial recognition and video analysis.

Chief Information Security Officer (CISO): An executive responsible for an organization's cybersecurity strategy and risk management.

Cloud Computing: The delivery of computing services such as storage, processing, and networking over the internet, allowing for scalable and flexible resource use.

Cloud Infrastructure: The underlying physical and virtual resources required for cloud computing, including servers, storage, and networking components.

Common Vulnerabilities and Exposures (CVE): A publicly available list of known cybersecurity vulnerabilities and exposures, maintained by MITRE, to standardize the identification of security issues.

Compliance: Adherence to laws, regulations, and guidelines that govern the operation of a business, particularly concerning data protection and cybersecurity.

Computer Emergency Response Team (CERT): A group of experts that responds to cybersecurity incidents, providing guidance and support to mitigate the impact of cyber threats.

Cryptojacking: The unauthorized use of someone's computer to mine cryptocurrency, often without the user's knowledge or consent.

Cyber Defense: The measures and strategies implemented to protect networks, systems, and data from cyber threats and attacks.

Cyber Threats: Malicious activities or actors that aim to disrupt, damage, or gain unauthorized access to computer systems and networks.

Cyber Threat Landscape: The evolving environment of potential threats and vulnerabilities that organizations must defend against in the digital space.

Cybercrime Syndicates: Organized groups of cybercriminals that operate like traditional criminal organizations but focus on cyber-related activities such as hacking, fraud, and data theft.

Cybersecurity: The practice of protecting systems, networks, and data from digital attacks, breaches, and unauthorized access.

Cybersecurity Posture: The overall strength and effectiveness of an organization's cybersecurity defenses and policies.

Cybersecurity Strategy: A comprehensive plan that outlines how an organization will protect its digital assets and respond to cyber threats.

Cybersecurity Tactics: The specific methods and techniques used to implement a cybersecurity strategy and protect against threats.

Data Analytics: The process of examining and interpreting complex data sets to inform decision-making and identify trends or patterns.

Data Breach: The unauthorized access, exposure, or theft of sensitive data, often resulting in significant financial and reputational damage.

Data Classification (DC): The process of categorizing data based on its sensitivity and value to ensure proper protection and compliance with security policies.

Data Encryption: The conversion of data into a secure code to prevent unauthorized access during transmission or storage.

Data Exfiltration: The unauthorized transfer of data from a computer or network, typically carried out by cybercriminals or malicious insiders.

Data Governance: The policies, procedures, and standards that ensure the proper management, quality, and security of data within an organization.

Data Integrity: The accuracy, consistency, and reliability of data throughout its lifecycle, ensuring it remains unaltered and trustworthy.

Data Mining: The process of analyzing large data sets to discover patterns, trends, and relationships that can inform business decisions.

Data Normalization: The process of organizing data to reduce redundancy and improve its structure, making it easier to analyze and use.

Data Preservation: The process of maintaining and protecting data over time to ensure its integrity, accessibility, and usability. It involves safeguarding data from loss, corruption, or unauthorized modifications, ensuring it remains available for future use.

Data Privacy: The protection of personal and sensitive information from unauthorized access, ensuring individuals' data rights are respected.

Data Processing Infrastructure: The hardware and software resources required to collect, store, and analyze data within an organization.

Deep Learning (DL): A subset of machine learning that uses multi-layered neural networks to detect patterns in large datasets, often applied in cybersecurity for threat detection and anomaly identification.

Data Loss Prevention (DLP): A set of security measures designed to prevent unauthorized access, sharing, or loss of sensitive data.

Deep Q-Network (DQN): A reinforcement learning algorithm that combines deep learning with Q-learning to enable AI agents to make optimal decisions in complex environments.

DevOps: A set of practices that combine software development (Dev) and IT operations (Ops) to shorten the development lifecycle and provide continuous delivery with high software quality.

DevSecOps: An extension of DevOps that integrates security practices into the DevOps workflow to ensure security is embedded throughout the software development and infrastructure management lifecycle.

Digital Forensics: The process of collecting, analyzing, and preserving digital evidence in a way that is legally permissible, often used in investigations of cybercrimes.

Digital Infrastructure: The collection of technologies and systems that support digital operations, including networks, data centers, and cloud services.

Ethical and Privacy Concerns: The considerations and potential issues related to the ethical use of technology and the protection of personal privacy.

Ethical Concerns: The moral principles and dilemmas that arise in the development and use of technology, particularly in AI and cybersecurity.

Endpoint Detection and Response (EDR): A cybersecurity technology that continuously monitors and responds to threats on endpoints such as laptops, desktops, and servers.

eXplainable AI (XAI): A branch of AI that focuses on making machine learning models transparent and interpretable, ensuring accountability in automated decision-making.

eXtended Detection and Response (XDR): A security technology that integrates multiple security products into a unified platform to improve threat detection, investigation, and response.

Exploit Detection: The identification of vulnerabilities or weaknesses in software or systems that cyber attackers could exploit.

False Positives and Negatives: Incorrect results produced by a security system; false positives indicate a threat where none exists, while false negatives fail to detect an actual threat.

False Positive Rate (FPR): The percentage of non-malicious events incorrectly identified as threats by a security system.

False Negative Rate (FNR): The percentage of actual threats that a security system fails to detect.

Foundation Model: A Foundation Model is a large-scale AI model that serves as the base for multiple AI applications. It is pre-trained on massive datasets and can be fine-tuned for specific tasks, such as cybersecurity automation.

Fraud Detection: The use of technology and algorithms to identify and prevent fraudulent activities, such as identity theft or financial fraud.

Fusion AI: The integration of multiple AI models or data sources to enhance decision-making, improve threat detection, and optimize cybersecurity operations.

General Data Protection Regulation (GDPR): A European Union regulation that governs the collection, use, and protection of personal data, with strict requirements and penalties for non-compliance.

Generative Adversarial Networks (GANs): A type of AI model where two neural networks compete against each other to generate realistic data, used for security testing and synthetic data creation.

Generative AI / GenAI: A type of artificial intelligence that can create new content, such as text, images, or code, based on learned patterns from training data.

Governance Framework: The structure and processes that guide decision-making and ensure accountability, particularly in managing data and technology.

Governance, Risk, and Compliance (GRC): A framework that helps organizations align IT with business goals while managing risk and ensuring compliance with regulations.

Historical Data: Previously collected data that is used for analysis, forecasting, and decision-making in various applications.

Health Insurance Portability and Accountability Act (HIPAA): A U.S. law that sets national standards for protecting sensitive patient health information from being disclosed without the patient's consent or knowledge.

Human-in-the-Loop (HITL) System: A system in which human input is required to guide or validate automated processes, particularly in AI decision-making.

Hyperautomation: The combination of AI, machine learning, and robotic process automation (RPA) to accelerate business processes and security workflows.

Infrastructure as Code (IaC): A method of managing and provisioning IT infrastructure through machine-readable configuration files, enabling automation, consistency, and scalability in deploying and maintaining systems.

Incident Management: The process of identifying, analyzing, and responding to security incidents to minimize damage and restore normal operations.

Incident Response: The actions taken to address and manage the aftermath of a security breach or cyberattack, aiming to minimize damage and restore operations.

IT Operations (ITOps): The processes and services managed by IT teams to maintain, optimize, and secure an organization's technology infrastructure and business systems.

Identity and Access Management (IAM): A framework of policies and technologies ensuring that only authorized users have access to an organization's critical information and resources.

Internet of Things (IoT): The network of physical devices, vehicles, appliances, and other objects embedded with sensors and software that enable them to connect and exchange data.

Internet Worm: A type of malicious software that replicates itself and spreads across networks, often causing widespread damage.

ISO 27001: An international standard for information security management systems (ISMS), providing a systematic approach to managing sensitive company information and ensuring its confidentiality, integrity, and availability.

Key Performance Indicators (KPIs): Measurable metrics used to evaluate the effectiveness of SOC operations and AI-driven security improvements.

Kindo: An AI-driven security operations platform that leverages autonomous AI agents to optimize SOC workflows, automate threat detection, and accelerate incident response.

Large Language Model (LLM): A Large Language Model (LLM) is an advanced artificial intelligence model trained on vast amounts of text data to understand and generate human-like language. LLMs can process natural language inputs, provide contextual responses, generate text, summarize information, and assist with decision-making. They are widely used in various applications, including cybersecurity, customer support, and automation, to enhance efficiency and streamline workflows.

Lateral Movement: A technique used by attackers to navigate through a network after gaining initial access, seeking valuable data or critical systems.

Local Interpretable Model-agnostic Explanations (LIME): LIME is an explainability technique that builds local surrogate models to approximate complex machine learning predictions. It works by perturbing input data and analyzing how the model's predictions change, providing insights into individual decisions.

Log Analysis: The process of reviewing and interpreting log files to identify security incidents, performance issues, or other relevant events.

Machine Learning (ML): A subset of AI that enables computers to learn from data and improve their performance over time without being explicitly programmed.

Machine Learning Algorithms: The mathematical models and statistical techniques used by machine learning systems to make predictions or decisions based on data.

Machine Learning Operations (MLOps): A practice that combines machine learning and DevOps principles to streamline the development, deployment, and monitoring of AI models.

Managed Security Service Provider (MSSP): A third-party service provider that offers outsourced monitoring and management of security devices and systems.

Malware: Malicious software designed to damage, disrupt, or gain unauthorized access to computer systems.

Mean Time to Detect (MTTD): The average time taken by a security system to detect a threat after it occurs.

Mean Time to Respond (MTTR): The average time taken to respond and mitigate a detected security incident.

Metaverse: A virtual space that combines augmented reality (AR), virtual reality (VR), and the internet, requiring robust security measures to protect digital identities and assets.

MITRE: A U.S.-based nonprofit organization that operates federally funded research and development centers (FFRDCs) and provides cybersecurity frameworks, including CVE and ATT&CK, to help organizations defend against cyber threats.

MITRE ATT&CK: A globally accessible knowledge base of adversary tactics, techniques, and procedures (TTPs) used by cybercriminals and threat actors, helping organizations improve their detection and response capabilities.

Morris Worm: The Morris Worm was one of the first worms distributed via the Internet, launched in 1988 by Robert Tappan Morris. It exploited vulnerabilities in Unix systems and caused widespread disruption, leading to the first conviction under the Computer Fraud and Abuse Act in the U.S.

Multi-Factor Authentication (MFA): A security mechanism that requires users to provide two or more verification factors to gain access to a system.

National Data Management Office (NDMO): A regulatory body in Saudi Arabia responsible for overseeing data governance, data classification, and data protection policies to ensure secure and efficient data management across organizations.

National Electronic Security Authority (NESA): The former cybersecurity authority in the UAE responsible for establishing and enforcing cybersecurity standards and policies for government and critical infrastructure organizations, now integrated into the UAE Cybersecurity Council.

National Institute of Standards and Technology (NIST): NIST is a U.S. federal agency that develops technology, metrics, and standards to enhance innovation and industrial competitiveness. In cybersecurity, NIST is known for its frameworks and guidelines, including the NIST Cybersecurity Framework.

Nation-State Actors: Nation-State Actors are government-sponsored entities that engage in cyber activities, including espionage, sabotage, or warfare, to further national interests.

Natural Language Processing (NLP): NLP is a branch of artificial intelligence that focuses on the interaction between computers and humans through natural language. In cybersecurity, NLP is used for threat intelligence, phishing detection, and analyzing large volumes of text data.

Network Devices: Network Devices are hardware components such as routers, switches, firewalls, and access points that are essential for network connectivity, security, and management.

Network Security Tools: These tools are software and hardware solutions designed to protect the network infrastructure by monitoring, detecting, and responding to security threats. Examples include firewalls, intrusion detection systems (IDS), and antivirus programs.

Network Segmentation: Network Segmentation is the practice of dividing a network into smaller, isolated segments to enhance security. It limits the spread of malware and restricts unauthorized access to sensitive data.

Network Traffic: Network Traffic refers to the data packets moving across a network at any given time. Monitoring and analyzing network traffic is crucial for identifying security threats and ensuring efficient network performance.

Neural Networks: A computational model inspired by the human brain, used in AI and machine learning to recognize patterns and make predictions.

No-Code Application Platform: A No-Code Application Platform allows users to create software applications through graphical user interfaces and configuration rather than traditional programming, enabling rapid development and deployment without deep technical expertise.

Operational Efficiency: Operational Efficiency refers to the ability of an organization to deliver its services or products in a cost-effective manner without compromising quality. In SOCs, it involves optimizing resources, processes, and tools to enhance security operations.

Operational Efficiencies: These are improvements made to operational processes that reduce waste, increase speed, and improve quality, leading to better overall performance in SOCs and other business functions.

Operational Technology (OT): Hardware and software that detect or cause changes in physical devices, processes, and events in industrial environments.

Payment Card Industry Data Security Standard (PCI DSS): A set of security standards designed to ensure that all companies that process, store, or transmit credit card information maintain a secure environment to protect cardholder data.

Penetration Testing (Pen Test): A simulated cyberattack conducted to evaluate the security of a system, network, or application by identifying vulnerabilities before malicious hackers can exploit them.

Performance Measurement: Performance Measurement involves tracking and evaluating the efficiency and effectiveness of an organization's activities, often through key performance indicators (KPIs) or metrics, to ensure that objectives are being met.

Personal Data Protection Law: Personal Data Protection Law encompasses legal frameworks designed to safeguard individuals' personal data from unauthorized access, use, or disclosure. Examples include the GDPR in Europe and the CCPA in California.

Phishing Attempts: Phishing Attempts are fraudulent efforts to obtain sensitive information by disguising it as a trustworthy entity in electronic communication, often leading to identity theft or financial loss.

Phishing Campaign: A Phishing Campaign is a coordinated attack involving multiple phishing attempts aimed at a specific target or group of targets to extract sensitive information or deploy malware.

Predictive Analysis: Predictive Analysis uses statistical algorithms, machine learning, and historical data to predict future events, trends, or behaviors. In cybersecurity, it helps anticipate potential threats and vulnerabilities.

Privileged Access Management (PAM): Security practices and tools designed to control and monitor access to sensitive systems and data by privileged users.

Proximal Policy Optimization (PPO): A reinforcement learning algorithm that optimizes policy performance by balancing exploration and exploitation, commonly used in AI-driven cybersecurity automation.

ProxyLogon: ProxyLogon refers to a set of critical vulnerabilities discovered in Microsoft Exchange servers in early 2021, which allowed attackers to execute arbitrary code and gain unauthorized access to emails and other sensitive data.

ProxyShell: ProxyShell is another set of vulnerabilities in Microsoft Exchange servers, disclosed in 2021, that allow remote code execution and are often exploited in conjunction with ProxyLogon.

Purple Teaming: A cybersecurity approach that combines the offensive tactics of red teams and the defensive strategies of blue teams to improve an organization's security posture.

Q-Learning: A reinforcement learning technique where an AI agent learns optimal actions by interacting with its environment and receiving feedback through rewards.

Quantum Computing: A revolutionary computing paradigm that leverages quantum mechanics to perform computations exponentially faster than classical computers, posing both opportunities and challenges for cybersecurity.

Quantum Cryptography: A security mechanism that uses quantum mechanics principles, such as quantum key distribution (QKD), to enable unbreakable encryption against future quantum attacks.

Reactive Position: A Reactive Position in cybersecurity refers to a strategy that focuses on responding to security incidents and threats after they occur rather than anticipating and preventing them proactively.

Red Teaming: An offensive security testing approach where ethical hackers simulate real-world cyberattacks to identify vulnerabilities in an organization's defenses.

Reinforcement Learning (RL): A machine learning technique in which an AI agent learns by interacting with its environment and receiving rewards for correct actions.

Ransomware: Ransomware is a type of malicious software designed to block access to a computer system or data, typically by encrypting files, until a ransom is paid by the victim.

Ransomware as a Service (RaaS): RaaS is a business model where ransomware developers lease their malware to other cybercriminals, allowing them to launch ransomware attacks without needing to create the software themselves.

Residual Errors: Residual Errors refer to the remaining errors or vulnerabilities in a system after mitigation efforts have been applied. These errors may still pose risks and require continuous monitoring.

Risk Management Procedures: Risk Management Procedures involve identifying, assessing, and prioritizing risks, followed by coordinated efforts to minimize, monitor, and control the probability or impact of unfortunate events.

Robotic Process Automation (RPA): A technology that uses software bots to automate repetitive, rule-based tasks in IT and business processes.

Sarbanes-OXley act (SOX): A U.S. federal law that mandates corporate financial transparency and includes provisions for IT security and controls.

Saudi Arabian Monetary Authority Cybersecurity Framework (SAMA CSF): A cybersecurity framework established by the Saudi Arabian Monetary Authority (SAMA) to enhance the security posture of financial institutions in Saudi Arabia. It provides guidelines for risk management, governance, and cybersecurity controls to ensure resilience against cyber threats.

SecOps: The collaboration between security and IT operations teams to improve security posture by streamlining incident detection, response, and mitigation.

Security Information and Event Management (SIEM): SIEM is a solution that provides real-time analysis of security alerts generated by network hardware and applications. It aggregates and correlates log data to help detect and respond to security incidents.

Security Orchestration, Automation, and Response (SOAR): SOAR refers to the integration of security tools, processes, and automation to improve the efficiency and effectiveness of security operations. It enables faster response times and better incident management.

Security Operation Centers (SOCs): SOCs are centralized units that monitor, detect, respond to, and manage cybersecurity incidents in real time. They play a critical role in protecting an organization's information assets.

Security Patches: Security Patches are updates released by software vendors to fix vulnerabilities, bugs, or security flaws in their products, helping to protect systems from cyber threats.

Security Tools: Security Tools are a broad category of software and hardware used to protect systems, networks, and data from cyber threats. Examples include antivirus software, firewalls, and encryption tools.

Self-Supervised Learning: An emerging AI training technique that allows models to learn from unlabeled data by generating their own training labels, improving efficiency in cybersecurity applications.

Service Interruptions: Service Interruptions occur when a service becomes temporarily unavailable, often due to technical issues, cyberattacks, or maintenance activities. Minimizing these interruptions is crucial for maintaining operational continuity.

SHAP (SHapley Additive Explanations): SHAP is an explainability method that assigns feature importance scores based on game theory. It helps interpret machine learning models by showing how each feature contributes to a prediction in a fair and consistent way.

Skills Gap: The Skills Gap in cybersecurity refers to the disparity between the skills required by employers and the skills possessed by the workforce, leading to challenges in hiring and maintaining effective security operations.

Small Language Model (SLM): A Small Language Model (SLM) is a lightweight AI model designed to process language with fewer computational resources and a more limited dataset compared to Large Language Models (LLMs). SLMs are optimized for efficiency, faster inference, and specific tasks, such as chatbot responses, on-device AI applications, and privacy-focused processing. While LLMs are powerful but resource-intensive, SLMs prioritize speed, cost-effectiveness, and operational constraints.

SOC Playbook: A SOC Playbook is a set of predefined procedures and guidelines that outline how to respond to specific types of cybersecurity incidents, ensuring a consistent and effective response across the organization.

SOC-as-a-Service (SOCaaS): SOCaaS is a managed service model where organizations outsource their SOC functions to third-party providers, allowing them to benefit from expert security monitoring and incident response without maintaining an in-house SOC.

SOC Maturity Model: A framework for assessing the effectiveness and readiness of a Security Operations Center, ranging from basic reactive monitoring to advanced proactive threat hunting.

Social Engineering: Social Engineering is the manipulation of individuals into performing actions or divulging confidential information, often through deception. It is a common tactic used in phishing and other cyberattacks.

State-Sponsored Cyber Warfare: State-Sponsored Cyber Warfare involves cyberattacks orchestrated by nation-states to disrupt, damage, or gain intelligence from other nations, often as part of broader geopolitical strategies.

Statistical Algorithms: Statistical Algorithms are mathematical formulas used to analyze data and make predictions or decisions based on statistical principles.

They are widely used in cybersecurity for threat detection and anomaly detection.

Strategic Cyber Defense: Strategic Cyber Defense involves long-term planning and implementation of security measures to protect an organization from advanced and persistent cyber threats, often focusing on resilience and proactive threat management.

Support Vector Machines (SVMs): SVMs are a type of supervised machine learning algorithm used for classification and regression tasks. In cybersecurity, they are often used for detecting anomalies, such as in intrusion detection systems.

Supplier Security Evaluations: Supplier Security Evaluations involve assessing the security practices and risks associated with third-party suppliers and vendors, ensuring they meet the organization's security standards.

Supervised Learning Algorithms: Supervised Learning Algorithms are a type of machine learning where the model is trained on labelled data. In cybersecurity, they are used to classify and predict threats based on historical data.

Synthetic Identity Fraud: A cybercrime tactic where attackers create fake identities using a combination of real and fabricated information to conduct fraud.

System Integrity: System Integrity refers to the assurance that a system and its data are protected from unauthorized alteration, ensuring that the system operates as intended and remains secure.

System Restoration: System Restoration involves returning a system to its normal operating state after a disruption, such as recovering data, restoring functionality, and ensuring security measures are re-established.

Tactics, Techniques, and Procedures (TTPs): A structured representation of the behavior and actions used by threat actors to execute cyberattacks, as categorized in frameworks like MITRE ATT&CK.

Text Analysis: Text Analysis is the process of extracting meaningful information from text data through techniques such as NLP, sentiment analysis, and pattern recognition. It is used in cybersecurity to analyze threat intelligence reports and identify phishing emails.

Threat Actor Profiling: Threat Actor Profiling involves analyzing the behavior, tools, and techniques of cybercriminals to predict and understand their future actions, helping organizations defend against targeted attacks.

Threat Detection: Threat Detection is the process of identifying potential security threats through monitoring, analyzing, and correlating data from various sources, such as network traffic, log files, and user behavior.

Threat Detection and Response (TDR): A cybersecurity approach that integrates detection and automated response mechanisms to mitigate security threats in real-time.

Threat Hunting: Threat Hunting is the proactive search for hidden threats within a network or system that have not yet been detected by automated tools, often involving advanced analysis and hypothesis testing.

Threat Intelligence: Threat Intelligence is the collection, analysis, and dissemination of information about current and emerging threats, helping organizations anticipate and defend against cyberattacks.

Threat Modeling: Threat Modeling is a structured approach to identifying and evaluating potential security threats to an organization's assets, helping to priorities and mitigate risks effectively.

Threat Scenario: A threat scenario is a hypothetical situation that describes how a particular threat could exploit vulnerabilities to cause harm. It is used in risk assessments and security planning.

Threat Triage: Threat Triage is the process of prioritizing security threats based on their severity, impact, and likelihood, enabling efficient allocation of resources to address the most critical issues first.

United Arab Emirates Information Assurance Standards (UAE IA): A cybersecurity framework issued by the UAE government to establish security controls, policies, and best practices for protecting critical information infrastructure and sensitive data within the country.

Unsupervised Learning Algorithms: Unsupervised Learning Algorithms are a type of machine learning that identifies patterns in data without labelled examples, often used for anomaly detection and clustering in cybersecurity.

User Behavior: User Behavior refers to the actions and patterns of activity exhibited by users within a network. Analyzing user behavior is crucial for detecting insider threats, compromised accounts, and unusual activities.

User LLM: A User LLM (Large Language Model) is an AI model that interacts directly with users, assisting them by answering queries, summarizing information, and providing context upon request. It requires human input to function and does not take independent actions. In a SOC, a User LLM helps analysts by offering insights, generating reports, and enriching incident data without making automated decisions.

Vulnerability: A vulnerability is a weakness or flaw in a system, network, or application that can be exploited by a threat actor to gain unauthorized access, disrupt services, or cause other harm.

Vulnerability Assessment: The process of identifying, quantifying, and prioritizing security weaknesses in a system, application, or network.

Vulnerability Response: Vulnerability Response involves identifying, prioritizing, and mitigating vulnerabilities in a timely manner to reduce the risk of exploitation and maintain system security.

Version Control: Version Control is the management of changes to documents, software code, or other collections of information, ensuring that previous versions can be retrieved, and changes can be tracked and managed.

Web 3.0: The next evolution of the internet, emphasizing decentralization, blockchain technology, and user sovereignty over data, enhancing security and privacy in digital interactions.

WhiteRabbitNeo: The first uncensored open-source AI model designed for cybersecurity automation, helping SOC, DevOps, and IT teams enhance threat intelligence, response, and automation.

Worker LLM: A Worker LLM is an AI model designed to operate autonomously in the background, performing tasks without needing direct user input. Unlike User LLMs, Worker LLMs can analyze alerts, correlate incidents, and even take automated response actions as part of security workflows. In a SOC, Worker LLMs enhances operational efficiency by reducing manual effort and responding to security threats in real time.

Zero-Day Exploits: Zero-Day Exploits are attacks that target vulnerabilities unknown to the software vendor or the public, giving defenders "zero days" to prepare or mitigate the threat.

Zero-Day Vulnerability: A Zero-Day Vulnerability is a security flaw in software that is unknown to the vendor and has no patch available, making it a prime target for attackers.

Zero-Trust Architectures: Zero-Trust Architectures are security models that operate on the principle of "never trust, always verify," where no user or device, inside or outside the network, is trusted by default.

References

Bi, A. S. (2023). What's important: The next academic — ChatGPT AI? Journal of Bone and Joint Surgery, American Volume. https://doi.org/10.2106/jbjs.23.00269

OpenAI. (2025). Threat intelligence report: Disrupting malicious uses of our models (February update). OpenAI. https://cdn.openai.com/threat-intelligence-reports/disrupting-malicious-uses-of-our-models-february-2025-update.pdf

Cloud backup archives. (n.d.). Tech Hero. https://techhero.com/tag/cloud-backup/

Anthropic. (2025). On the feasibility of using LLMs to execute multistage network attacks. Anthropic Research. https://www.anthropic.com/research/llm-multistage-network-attacks

Nvidia. (2024). Jensen Huang on cybersecurity: Our cybersecurity system today can't run without agents. BG2 Podcast. https://www.bg2podcast.com/nvidia-huang-cybersecurity-agents

Claroty unveils zero-infrastructure cybersecurity solution to protect industrial enterprises. (2021). The Manufacturing Connection. https://themanufacturingconnection.com/2021/06/claroty-unveils-zero-infrastructure-cybersecurity-solution-to-protect-industrial-enterprises/

Dande, A. A., & Pund, M. A. (2023). A review study on applications of natural language processing. International Journal of Scientific Research in Science, Engineering and Technology. https://doi.org/10.32628/ijsrset2310214

The impact of artificial intelligence on employment and job roles. (2023). Zenodo. https://doi.org/10.5281/zenodo.8287470

Understanding predictive marketing: Anticipating consumer behavior with AI. (n.d.). SEO Outsourcing. https://seooutsourcing.com/ai-in-predictive-marketing-2/

OpenAI. (2025). OSTP AI Action Plan response letter: Requesting cybersecurity support for AI labs. OpenAI Official Communications. https://www.openai.com/ostp-ai-action-plan-response

Council on Foreign Relations. (2025). CEO Event: Securing AI Labs and Protecting Algorithmic Data – Insights by Dario Amodei, CEO of Anthropic. Council on Foreign Relations Events. https://www.cfr.org/events/securing-ai-labs-dario-amodei

Darktrace ActiveAI Security Platform™ provides a full lifecycle of threat detection and response. (2024). Darktrace. https://ir.darktrace.com/press-releases/2024/4/9/ad92f587789affc79165e131f0e4d8752139a9b7d960c0c148a888da891b071d#:~:text=The%20Darktrace%20ActiveAI%20Security%20Platform%E2%84%A2%20provides%20a%20full%20lifecycle,to%20known%20and%20unknown%20in

CrowdStrike Falcon platform utilizes AI to stay ahead of adversaries. (n.d.). CrowdStrike. https://www.crowdstrike.com/cybersecurity-101/artificial-intelligence/#:~:text=The%20Falcon%20platform%20utilizes%20AI,to%20stay%20ahead%20of%20adversaries

Microsoft Security. (2022). Microsoft Exchange vulnerabilities: Understanding ProxyShell and ProxyLogon. Microsoft.

https://www.microsoft.com/security/blog/2022/01/01/ex
change-vulnerabilities

ZDNet. (2022). Exploiting Microsoft Exchange: A case study
on ProxyShell and ProxyLogon. ZDNet.
https://www.zdnet.com/article/microsoft-exchange-
exploits

Maximizing the benefits of Hyperautomation in security
through SOAR platform. (n.d.). SIRP.
https://www.sirp.io/blog/maximizing-the-benefits-of-
hyperautomation-in-security-through-soar-platform/

Google DeepMind. (2024). From naptime to big sleep: AI
discovers security vulnerabilities. Google Project Zero.
https://googleprojectzero.blogspot.com/2024/10/from-
naptime-to-big-sleep.html

MIT CSAIL. (2024). Modeling adversarial intelligence to
exploit AI's security vulnerabilities. MIT Computer Science &
Artificial Intelligence Laboratory.
https://www.csail.mit.edu/news/3-questions-modeling-
adversarial-intelligence-exploit-ais-security-vulnerabilities

Darktrace. (2024). Cyber AI: Autonomous threat detection and response. Darktrace Reports. https://www.darktrace.com/en/cyber-ai-threat-detection

CrowdStrike. (2024). AI in cybersecurity: Revolutionizing threat detection. CrowdStrike Research. https://www.crowdstrike.com/blog/ai-cybersecurity-trend

Microsoft Security. (2024). Leveraging AI to secure digital environments. Microsoft Security Reports. https://www.microsoft.com/en-us/security/blog/ai-in-cybersecurity

Google DeepMind & MIT CSAIL. (2024). Reducing cyberattacks containment times from hours to minutes using AI. AI Security Journal. https://www.deepmind.com/research/ai-security-response-time

The panel on personal data protection bills will submit a report to Parliament's Winter Session. (n.d.). Livemint. https://www.livemint.com/news/india/panel-on-personal-data-protection-bill-to-submit-report-in-parliament-s-winter-session-11600867886634.html

Building a stronger security culture with security education programs. (n.d.). Top Antivirus Site Reviews. https://top10antivirus.site/building-a-stronger-security-culture-with-security-education-programs/

Bank of America's Erica AI surpassed 15 billion client interactions: Here's what that means for the future of AI in banking. (n.d.). Future Digital Finance. https://futuredigitalfinance.wbresearch.com/blog/bank-of-americas-erica-ai-surpassed-15-billion-client-interactions-heres-what-that-means-for-the-future-of-ai-in-banking#:~:text=Another%20example%20can%20be%20found,transaction%20data%20to%20identify%20and

Cybersecurity Ventures. (2023). MOVEit Transfer data breach: Analysis and implications. Cybersecurity Ventures. https://www.cybersecurityventures.com/moveit-data-breach

ThreatPost. (2023). MOVEit Transfer breach exposes sensitive data from high-profile targets. ThreatPost. https://www.threatpost.com/moveit-transfer-breach

Amazon Fraud Detector uses machine learning to identify potentially fraudulent activities. (n.d.). Amazon Web

Services.   https://aws.amazon.com/fraud-
detector/faqs/#:~:text=Amazon%20Fraud%20Detector%20u
ses%20machine,and%20Amazon.com%20to%20automaticall
y

The impact of social media on employee recruitment and
branding.   (n.d.).   AlignMark.
https://www.alignmark.com/the-impact-of-social-media-
on-employee-recruitment-and-branding/

Walmart's AI-powered inventory system brightens the
holidays.   (n.d.).   Walmart   Global   Tech.
https://tech.walmart.com/content/walmart-global-
tech/en_us/blog/post/walmarts-ai-powered-inventory-
system-brightens-the-holidays.html

Google Threat Intelligence Group. (2025). Adversarial misuse
of generative AI: How threat actors leverage GenAI in
cyberattacks.   Google   Threat   Intelligence   Report.
https://cloud.google.com/blog/topics/threat-
intelligence/adversarial-misuse-generative-ai

MIT Technology Review. (2023). The dark side of AI: How
cybercriminals weaponize artificial intelligence. MIT
Technology Review.

https://www.technologyreview.com/2023/11/05/the-dark-side-of-ai-cybercrime

IBM Security. (2024). AI and cybercrime: The rise of machine-learning-powered attacks. IBM X-Force Threat Intelligence Report. https://www.ibm.com/security/ai-cybercrime

Gartner. (2023). Emerging AI-powered threats and their implications for enterprise security. Gartner Security Insights. https://www.gartner.com/en/research/ai-cyber-threats

F-Secure Labs. (2023). The role of generative AI in cyberattacks: Risks and mitigations. F-Secure Research. https://labs.f-secure.com/research/genai-threats

Microsoft Threat Intelligence. (2024). AI-enhanced threat detection: How machine learning revolutionizes SOC operations. Microsoft Security Blog. https://www.microsoft.com/security/blog/ai-threat-detection

Splunk. (2023). AI-driven security analytics: Enhancing SOC threat detection and response. Splunk Security Insights. https://www.splunk.com/en_us/blog/security/ai-driven-threat-detection.html

Palo Alto works. (2024). The future of cybersecurity: AI in threat detection and incident response. Palo Alto Networks Research. https://www.paloaltonetworks.com/research/ai-security

Fortinet. (2023). AI-powered threat intelligence: Automating threat detection for modern SOCs. Fortinet Threat Landscape Report. https://www.fortinet.com/reports/ai-cybersecurity

Elastic Security. (2023). Machine learning in cybersecurity: How AI is transforming SOCs. Elastic Threat Intelligence. https://www.elastic.co/security/ai-threat-intelligence

Accenture Security. (2024). Thriving in an AI-driven SOC: The role of autonomous agents. Accenture Cybersecurity Report. https://www.accenture.com/us-en/insights/security/ai-soc

Forrester Research. (2023). AI and automation in cybersecurity: Strategies for thriving in the new era. Forrester Security Trends. https://www.forrester.com/research/ai-cybersecurity-trends

Darktrace. (2024). AI and autonomous SOCs: Reducing analyst workload and improving security outcomes.

Darktrace   Research.
https://www.darktrace.com/insights/ai-autonomous-socs

McAfee Security. (2023). How autonomous agents improve
cybersecurity   resilience.   McAfee   Labs   Research.
https://www.mcafee.com/blogs/security-news/ai-in-
cybersecurity

RSA Security. (2024). AI-driven SOC evolution: How
automation and machine learning redefine cybersecurity.
RSA Threat Intelligence. https://www.rsa.com/security-ai

NIST. (2023). Future trends in AI-enabled cybersecurity: A
roadmap for SOC evolution. National Institute of Standards
and   Technology   (NIST).
https://www.nist.gov/cybersecurity/ai-soc-future

Bono, J., Grana, J., & Xu, A. (2024). Generative AI and Security
Operations Center Productivity: Evidence from Live
Operations. arXiv. https://arxiv.org/html/2411.03116v2

Cassetto, O. (2024). AI SOC: The Definition and Components
of   AI-Driven   SOC.   Radiant   Security.
https://radiantsecurity.ai/learn/ai-driven-soc/

Gregory, J. (2025). How AI-Driven SOC Co-Pilots Will Change Security Center Operations. Security Intelligence. https://securityintelligence.com/articles/how-ai-driven-soc-co-pilots-will-change-security-center-operations/

Gurucul. (2024). ML and AI in Modern Security Operations Center. Gurucul Blog. https://gurucul.com/blog/role-machine-learning-ai-modern-security-operations-center/

Moore, S. (2024). SOC and SIEM: The Role of SIEM Solutions in the SOC. Exabeam. https://www.exabeam.com/explainers/siem-security/the-soc-secops-and-siem/

Netenrich. (2025). Engineering Intelligence: Why AI Alone Will Not Build Future-Ready SOCs (And What Will). Netenrich Blog. https://netenrich.com/blog/engineering-intelligence-why-ai-alone-will-not-build-future-ready-socs-and-what-will

Palo Alto Networks. (2024). How AI-Driven SOC Solutions Transform Cybersecurity: Cortex XSIAM. Palo Alto Networks Cyberpedia. https://www.paloaltonetworks.co.uk/cyberpedia/revolutionizing-soc-operations-with-ai-soc-solutions

PwC. (2024). What is the Future of Security Operations (SecOps). PwC. https://www.pwc.com/us/en/technology/alliances/library/google-future-of-secops.html

Cybersecurity & Infrastructure Security Agency (CISA). (2024). AI-driven cybersecurity: The evolving landscape. CISA Threat Reports. https://www.cisa.gov/ai-security

Trend Micro. (2023). The next decade of AI-enabled security: Future trends and innovations. Trend Micro Security Research. https://www.trendmicro.com/ai-security-future

Kaspersky Labs. (2024). AI and cybersecurity in 2030: Predicting future attack vectors. Kaspersky Security Bulletin. https://www.kaspersky.com/insights/ai-future-trends

Gartner. (2024). The future of AI-driven cybersecurity: Trends, challenges, and opportunities. Gartner Cybersecurity Forecasts. https://www.gartner.com/en/research/ai-cyber-future

MIT Sloan Management Review. (2024). The power of predictive analytics in cybersecurity: Trends and applications. MIT Sloan Review.

https://mitsloanreview.com/cybersecurity-predictive-analytics

Carnegie Mellon University. (2023). AI-driven predictive analytics for proactive cyber defense. Software Engineering Institute (SEI). https://sei.cmu.edu/research/predictive-ai-cybersecurity

Palo Alto Networks. (2024). AI and predictive threat intelligence: A new frontier in cybersecurity. Palo Alto Networks Research. https://www.paloaltonetworks.com/predictive-ai-security

NIST. (2023). The role of machine learning in predictive threat modeling. National Institute of Standards and Technology (NIST). https://www.nist.gov/cybersecurity/ml-predictive-threats

McAfee Security. (2024). Predictive analytics for cyber resilience: How AI anticipate security breaches. McAfee Threat Research. https://www.mcafee.com/predictive-cybersecurity

Cisco Talos. (2023). AI-driven behavioral analytics in cyber defense: Lessons from global attacks. Cisco Talos Research. https://talosintelligence.com/research/ai-behavioral-cyber

Accenture Security. (2024). Future-proofing cybersecurity: The role of AI in predictive defense. Accenture Research. https://www.accenture.com/predictive-security

Harvard Business Review. (2023). Proactive cybersecurity with AI: Leveraging predictive analytics for better protection. Harvard Business Review. https://hbr.org/cybersecurity-ai-predictive

KPMG Cyber. (2024). AI-powered SOC efficiency: Optimizing operations with automation. KPMG Cybersecurity Report. https://www.kpmg.com/ai-soc-efficiency

Deloitte Insights. (2023). The future of SOC automation: AI, orchestration, and predictive insights. Deloitte Cyber Risk Services. https://www2.deloitte.com/ai-soc-operations

PwC Security. (2024). AI-driven SOCs: Reducing operational overhead through intelligent automation. PwC Cybersecurity Report. https://www.pwc.com/soc-ai-automation

IBM X-Force. (2023). Operational efficiencies in AI-driven SOCs: Best practices for automation. IBM Security Research. https://www.ibm.com/xforce/ai-soc-operations

Microsoft Security. (2024). How AI optimizes security operations: The role of automation in modern SOCs. Microsoft Cybersecurity Insights. https://www.microsoft.com/security/ai-soc-automation

Google Cloud Security. (2023). AI-enhanced SOC workflows: Streamlining incident management and response. Google Security Blog. https://cloud.google.com/security/ai-soc-efficiency

Verizon Cyber Intelligence. (2024). SOC modernization: AI and machine learning for enhanced threat response. Verizon Data Breach Investigations Report (DBIR). https://www.verizon.com/cybersecurity/ai-soc

EY Cybersecurity. (2023). Leveraging AI for operational efficiency in security operations centers. EY Security Advisory. https://www.ey.com/soc-ai-optimization

European Union Agency for Cybersecurity (ENISA). (2024). Ethical AI in cybersecurity: Legal frameworks and best practices. ENISA Report on AI Ethics. https://www.enisa.europa.eu/ai-ethics

National Institute of Standards and Technology (NIST). (2023). AI risk management framework: Addressing bias, accountability, and transparency. NIST AI Risk Guidelines. https://www.nist.gov/ai-risk-framework

Cybersecurity and Infrastructure Security Agency (CISA). (2024). AI ethics in security operations: A guide for government and enterprise SOCs. CISA Threat Intelligence Report. https://www.cisa.gov/ai-ethics-cybersecurity

Future of Privacy Forum (FPF). (2023). The intersection of AI and data privacy laws: A global perspective. Future Privacy Research Journal. https://fpf.org/ai-data-privacy

IEEE Standards Association. (2023). Ethical considerations in AI-powered security systems. IEEE AI Ethics Report. https://standards.ieee.org/ai-ethics-security

United Nations Office on Drugs and Crime (UNODC). (2024). AI and cybercrime: Legal and regulatory challenges. UNODC Cybercrime Report. https://www.unodc.org/ai-cybercrime-regulations

Harvard Law Review. (2023). AI-driven cybersecurity and the law: Liability and accountability in automated SOCs. Harvard Law & Technology Journal. https://hls.harvard.edu/ai-cybersecurity-law

MIT Sloan Management Review. (2024). AI-human collaboration in cybersecurity: The role of trust and transparency. MIT Sloan Review. https://mitsloanreview.com/ai-human-soc

Carnegie Mellon University - Software Engineering Institute (SEI). (2023). The future of human-AI teamwork in SOCs. CMU SEI Research. https://sei.cmu.edu/human-ai-collaboration

Google DeepMind. (2024). Enhancing human decision-making in SOCs with AI-assisted workflows. Google Research. https://deepmind.google/research/ai-human-soc

Navigating data privacy compliance for transcription. (n.d.). Way with Words. https://waywithwords.net/resource/data-privacy-compliance-transcription/

Darktrace. (2023). The evolution of AI-assisted SOCs: How analysts and AI work together. Darktrace Research. https://www.darktrace.com/ai-soc-human-partnership

Accenture Security. (2024). AI-augmented SOCs: The role of human-machine teaming. Accenture Cybersecurity Insights. https://www.accenture.com/ai-soc-human-machine

Forrester Research. (2023). Human-in-the-loop AI: Best practices for security teams. Forrester AI Research. https://www.forrester.com/human-ai-soc

McKinsey & Company. (2024). The AI-powered SOC: Blending human expertise with automation. McKinsey Digital Security Report. https://www.mckinsey.com/ai-human-soc

Gartner. (2024). Implementing AI in SOCs: A strategic guide for CISOs. Gartner Security Insights. https://www.gartner.com/research/ai-soc-implementation

IBM Security. (2023). AI-driven SOC implementation: Lessons from global deployments. IBM X-Force Research. https://www.ibm.com/security/ai-soc-best-practices

PwC Cybersecurity. (2024). Deploying AI in SOCs: Frameworks and key considerations. PwC Cybersecurity Report. https://www.pwc.com/ai-soc-deployment

Microsoft Security. (2023). How to integrate AI into existing SOC workflows. Microsoft AI Security Blog. https://www.microsoft.com/security/ai-soc-integration

Elastic Security. (2024). Building AI-powered SOCs: Key takeaways from real-world deployments. Elastic Security Insights. https://www.elastic.co/security/ai-soc-deployment

Splunk. (2023). Scaling AI-driven security operations: Best practices and use cases. Splunk Security Blog. https://www.splunk.com/ai-soc-scaling

CIS Benchmarks. (2024). AI in cybersecurity operations: A compliance-first approach. Center for Internet Security (CIS) Report. https://www.cisecurity.org/ai-soc-compliance

Streamlining patient outcomes with AI (in senior healthcare) (10 important questions answered). (n.d.). Senior Care Franchise   Info.

413

https://seniorcarefranchiseinfo.org/streamlining-patient-outcomes-with-ai-in-senior-healthcare/

The basics of continuing education for HVAC contractors. (2022). Opexi. https://opexi.net/2022/11/05/the-basics-of-continuing-education-for-hvac-contractors-continuing-education-schools/

International Cybersecurity Agency. (2023). The SolarWinds attack and its impact on cybersecurity. Retrieved from https://www.internationalcybersecurityagency.org/solarwinds-attack

WhiteRabbitNeo: An Uncensored, Open-Source AI Model for Red and Blue Team Cybersecurity. (2024). WhiteRabbitNeo Official Website. https://www.whiterabbitneo.com/

Kindo: Enterprise-Ready Agentic Security with Gen AI and Autonomous Agents. (2024). Kindo Official Website. https://www.kindo.ai/

Pair Hacking and Defending with WhiteRabbitNeo AI + Kindo Dev Copilot. (2024). Kindo Blog. https://www.kindo.ai/blog/pair-hacking-and-defending-with-whiterabbitneo-ai-kindo-dev-copilot

WhiteRabbitNeo: High-Powered Potential of Uncensored AI Pen testing for Attackers and Defenders. (2024). SecurityWeek. https://www.securityweek.com/whiterabbitneo-high-powered-potential-of-uncensored-ai-pentesting-for-attackers-and-defenders/

Kindo Raises $20.6M to Bring Security to Enterprise AI. (2024). VentureBeat. https://venturebeat.com/ai/kindo-raises-20-6m-to-bring-security-to-enterprise-ai/

WhiteRabbitNeo Releases New Version. (2024). DEVOPSdigest. https://www.devopsdigest.com/whiterabbitneo-releases-new-version

Kindo: The Story Behind This Rapidly Growing AI Security Company. (2024). Pulse 2.0. https://pulse2.com/kindo-bryan-vann-ron-williams-profile/

Open Source GenAI Model WhiteRabbitNeo Advances Support for Offensive Cybersecurity and DevSecOps Teams with New Release. (2024). GlobeNewswire. https://www.globenewswire.com/news-release/2024/10/23/2967886/0/en/Open-Source-GenAI-

Model-WhiteRabbitNeo-Advances-Support-for-Offensive-Cybersecurity-and-DevSecOps-Teams-with-New-Release.html

WhiteRabbitNeo: An Uncensored, Open-Source AI Model for Red Teamers and Cybersecurity Professionals. (2024). Taico.ca. https://taico.ca/posts/whiterabbitneo/

White Rabbit Neo AI: How AI is Revolutionizing Cybersecurity. (2024). Rich Washburn Blog. https://www.richwashburn.com/post/white-rabbit-neo-ai-how-ai-is-revolutionizing-cybersecurity

WhiteRabbitNeo/WhiteRabbitNeo-33B-v1.5. (2024). Hugging Face. https://huggingface.co/WhiteRabbitNeo/WhiteRabbitNeo-33B-v1.5

www.ingramcontent.com/pod-product-compliance
Lightning Source LLC
LaVergne TN
LVHW051220050326
832903LV00028B/2178